Customer Retention

Also available from ASQC Quality Press

Measuring Customer Satisfaction:
Development and Use of Questionnaires
Bob E. Hayes

Creating a Customer-Centered Culture:
Leadership in Quality, Innovation, and Speed
Robin L. Lawton

The Service/Quality Solution:
Using Service Management to Gain
Competitive Advantage
David A. Collier

Managing the Four Stages of TQM:
How to Achieve World-Class Performance
Charles N. Weaver

The ASQC Total Quality Management Series

> *TQM: Leadership for the Quality Transformation*
> Richard S. Johnson
>
> *TQM: Management Processes for Quality Operations*
> Richard S. Johnson
>
> *TQM: The Mechanics of Quality Processes*
> Richard S. Johnson and Lawrence E. Kazense
>
> *TQM: Quality Training Practices*
> Richard S. Johnson

To request a complimentary catalog of publications, call 800-248-1946.

Customer Retention

*An Integrated Process for Keeping
Your Best Customers*

Michael W. Lowenstein

ASQC Quality Press
Milwaukee, Wisconsin

Customer Retention: An Integrated Process for Keeping Your Best Customers
Michael W. Lowenstein

Library of Congress Cataloging-in-Publication Data
Lowenstein, Michael W., 1942–
    Customer retention: an integrated process for keeping your best
customers / Michael W. Lowenstein.
      p. cm.
    Includes bibliographical references and index.
    ISBN 0-87389-257-7 (acid-free paper)
    1. Consumer satisfaction. 2. Customer relations. 3. Customer
service. I. Title.
    HF5415.32.L69   1995
    658.8'12—dc20
                      94-46192
                      CIP

10 9 8 7 6 5 4 3 2 1

ISBN 0-87389-257-7

ASQC Mission: To facilitate continuous improvement and increase customer satisfaction by identifying, communicating, and promoting the use of quality principles, concepts, and technologies; and thereby be recognized throughout the world as the leading authority on, and champion for, quality.

For a free copy of the ASQC Quality Press Publications Catalog, including ASQC membership information, call 800-248-1946.

Printed in the United States of America

 Printed on acid-free recycled paper

 ASQC
Quality Press
611 East Wisconsin Avenue
Milwaukee, Wisconsin 53202

To Joanna, Shari, Mom and Dad,
and Ron and Judy

. . . and Susan

Two roads diverged in a woods, and I—
I took the one less traveled by,
and that has made all the difference.

Robert Frost
"The Road Not Taken"

Contents

Preface

Accompanying the increasing awareness of quality as an end goal for U.S. business, more and more companies have found a new icon: *customer satisfaction*. Virtually everywhere, companies ballyhoo their version of the credo: "number 1 in customer satisfaction" or "guaranteed satisfaction."

With this awareness comes the instructors, consultants, academics, and other experts of customer satisfaction, offering endless variations of seminar/conference/tutorial/course and folksy how-to books. Hardly a week goes by that some organization doesn't send a new customer satisfaction seminar brochure or some publisher doesn't announce a new customer satisfaction book.

So the attention surrounding customer satisfaction must really be helping U.S. companies provide superior customer service, right? Here's the reality. A recent study by Ernst & Young and the American Quality Foundation[1] showed that on key components of service excellence—employee involvement, complaint monitoring, use of service performance measurement devices by senior management—major service industries in the United States perform poorly, especially when compared to their counterparts overseas.

Taizo Watanabe, former director general for public information of the Japanese Foreign Ministry and a keen observer of U.S. business performance, made a particularly incisive comment in a recent interview.

> When I was watching the movie *Back to the Future,* I was surprised to see that the U.S. in the '50s and Japan now share similar characteristics. People jumped to wash your windshield and so on. But nobody does that in the U.S. today. In Japan, they still do. Something has changed in the U.S. in the course of time.[2]

Clearly, providing excellent customer service can be a powerful quality tool for any business. But satisfying, even delighting, customers may not be enough to keep them. And if all competitors are driving toward objectives like "100% customer satisfaction," why do customers still go elsewhere? Here is where most businesses and service performance evaluations miss a most salient point: *Customer retention requires a different mind-set and different measurement tools than customer satisfaction.*

As Watanabe's description of the state of customer service in the United States discusses, satisfaction is a passive and benign relationship with the customer, while retention is proactive and dynamic.

The mission of this book is to suggest and support a fresh perspective for product and service providers. That perspective is customer retention or customer loyalty, in addition to, or rather than, customer satisfaction.

While satisfaction, as a concept, provides an initial focus for companies pursuing a quality initiative, customer retention represents a dramatically more cost-effective, positive culture-building, profitable, and quality-centered set of activities. This is not merely a thesis, it is a fact. And this book will outline and cite numerous examples of the advantages of a customer-retention focus.

The ultimate challenge of service and product quality is to concentrate limited corporate resources—time, money, staff, and facilities—where they will have the greatest impact in keeping customers loyal. To help meet that challenge, the measurement and analysis of customers' requirements and perceptions also needs to be concentrated on knowing what it takes to keep (and lose) the best, most profitable customers. With this valuable information in hand, corporations should effectively deploy retention data throughout the organization so that everyone, from the chairperson to the file clerk, understands what each must contribute in order to keep customers.

Michael Lowenstein
February 1994

Notes

1. Gilbert Fuchsberg, "Quality Programs Show Shoddy Results," *The Wall Street Journal*, 14 May 1992, B1, B7.

2. Divina Infusino, "Taizo Watanabe: Japan's Voice to the World Discusses Common Ground," *Vis a Vis* (April 1992): 62+.

Acknowledgments

Gichin Funakoshi, the Okinawan who is revered around the world as the father of modern martial arts, wrote in his autobiography: "When a person enters upon an undertaking, he knows he needs the help of others; success is not to be attained alone."

The effort of writing a book, often solitary, was made easier by the support and help of colleagues like Abraham Wolf, Ph.D., president of ARBOR, Inc.; Gabriel Ross, Ph.D., president of ARBOR's Education and Training Division; Tom Lutz and David Saunders of ARBOR's Total Quality Group; and Craig Cunningham, formerly of ARBOR. Special thanks to David for the concept of Plan, Gather, Understand, and Deploy; to Craig for sharing his ideas on VOC assessment and planning and for reactive and indirect data gathering methods; and to Tom for the Verbatim Analysis Card[SM] idea, which is included in chapter 12. I would also like to thank Mark Cary, Ph.D., formerly vice president of statistical analysis at ARBOR, for his advice on statistical interpretation; John Fava, senior project director at ARBOR, for suggesting an alternative data modeling approach; and to Roger Taylor, M.D., Thom Clopton, Sc.D., and Ben Singer of Pacificare for taking time to review their 'Art of Caring' program and how they benefit from the concept of touch. Additionally, my thanks to Terry Bounds, who not only typed most of the manuscript, but helpfully shared her impressions as she typed.

In a different way, I would like to thank my martial arts instructors over the years—Master Young H. Kwon, Master Mark Causerano, Master Jhoon Rhee, and especially Grandmaster Jae Chul Shin—and those whose ideas and writing, some contemporary and some over 2000 years old, helped guide my path.

Lastly, I would like to thank my daughter Joanna, who, although not totally comprehending either the book's subject or my zeal for it, encouraged me throughout the writing process.

Introduction

Today, many companies find themselves in a rapid state of transition. Customers are giving these companies powerful wake-up calls—usually with their money as the alarm clock—that offering the best products, services, or prices alone may not be enough to ensure loyalty. As a result, companies have tried to identify what their customers want and then set up satisfaction programs accordingly.

Often, assuming that customers are satisfied has seemed to be a panacea for maintaining or increasing sales, but the concept and drive for satisfied customers generally have proven far less than satisfactory for companies seeking higher sales and profits, greater quality levels, and more cultural cohesion among staff. These objectives are more capable of being met when activities and resources are applied around the concept of customer retention.

This book first introduces the reader to the concept of customer retention, by itself and relative to customer satisfaction; discusses its components; and then applies its theses to sales and marketing decision making, training, culture building, and continuous quality improvement.

Readers may find it helpful to have a thumbnail sketch of each chapter beforehand. The following is a chapter-by-chapter summary.

Chapter 1: The Myth of Customer Satisfaction

Companies tend to concentrate their resources on acquiring and satisfying customers without sufficient understanding of what it takes to keep customers (and staff) loyal. Popular belief, and much of the writing and thinking about customers, centers around having them satisfied. This even extends to prestigious awards like the Malcolm Baldrige National Quality Award, which stresses customer satisfaction. The reality is, however, that customers who say they are satisfied are often just as likely to be disloyal as other customers.

Chapter 2: Customer Satisfaction vs. Customer Retention

The relationship between customer satisfaction and customer retention depends, at least in part, on what outcomes companies desire.

Satisfaction is a less than reliable indicator of customer loyalty because it tends to be more passive than proactive. Retention-centered companies focus on customers who may be planning to defect. They also gain insight from former customers and internal customers.

Complaints represent a clear departure from a reactive customer satisfaction approach. Rather than wait to hear from the small proportion of customers who complain, retention-centered companies seek out the latent, or unspoken, complaints from all customers, particularly those who may defect.

Chapter 3: The Six Failures and Five Cures of Customer Product and Service Performance Measurement

Product and service performance measurement systems frequently provide too little direction because they yield tactical, general, reactive report cards that don't consider customer needs and expectations, and don't include staff as customers. Proactive measurement systems overcome these deficiencies, look at service transactions, and generate action-oriented models for keeping customers.

Chapter 4: Evaluating Latent and Registered Complaints

Registered complaint systems, though the predominant method companies use to capture complaint data, literally represent only the tip of the complaint iceberg. Companies must generate latent, or unregistered, complaints through direct customer contact or modifications to their customer measurement systems. Complaints and their resolution frequently impact customer loyalty, so it is important to act on them, especially those correlating with potential customer loss.

Chapter 5: Identifying Customer Needs, Expectations, and Problems and Gauging Their Impact

Customer needs, expectations, and problems must be identified and assessed on a systematized, continuous basis. Customers make trade-offs in every supplier, product, or service selection process. Companies understanding these trade-offs and how they impact customer decisions will be able to offer products and services accordingly.

Chapter 6: Customer-Provider Gaps

One key reason for customer attrition and loss is companies' inability to align the delivery of their products, services, or staff performance with the attitude of the customer. In other words, they do not understand how direct the correlation is between alignment and retention. Opportunity for alignment or misalignment especially occurs during customer-provider sales/service transactions, or deliveries—places in which provider and recipient touch. Methods exist for proactively narrowing or eliminating gaps.

Chapter 7: What Is the Competition Doing?

In addition to understanding customers, companies should also continuously monitor competitive activities. Much like battle strategies or a chess game, the offensive, defensive, and flanking moves very much depend on marketplace position at the time. Companies develop information on their relative competitive position by asking current and former customers, and from noncustomers through direct observation and other gathering techniques.

Chapter 8: Planning for Research, Developing Research Instruments, and Meaningfully Reporting Customer Service Research Results

Central to a customer information system (CIS) is the customer research program itself. Depending on several factors—company culture, marketplace dynamism, competition, research budget—companies decide the who, what, where, and how of conducting customer research. With a basic plan, companies can structure questionnaires, analyses, and reports to help meet their customer loyalty objectives.

Chapter 9: Customer Retention Modeling

Models are developed and used to help companies allocate their service time, money, staff, and facilities through prioritized activities. Without well-constructed and interpreted models, they would be faced with the same problem confronting many other companies collecting "satisfaction" data. While many techniques purport to be models of customer behavior (Customer Satisfaction Index, Customer Satisfaction Quotient, and so on), only those built around customer loyalty enable companies to prioritize which activities and performance areas need attention and resources.

Chapter 10: Effectively Deploying Customer Data Throughout the Organization

Deployment may be the most important element of a CIS, and the most neglected. Actionable customer data are the foundation of effective deployment. Use of step models—quality function deployment (QFD), Hoshin, and analytic hierarchy process (AHP)—are three quality-based methods of deploying information; but, above all, companies must concentrate on getting information to those who deal most directly with customers. Information must focus on positive change in behaviors, actions, and deliveries.

Chapter 11: Kaizen and the Japanese Approach to Customer Retention: Lessons for U.S. Business

Kaizen is the Japanese concept of continuous, lifelong improvement. It is reflected in their art, trade, products, marketing, and customer service. Japanese companies frequently offer extraordinary customer support and service, while at the same time expending little energy in things that don't help them retain desirable customers. As an illustration, their market research tends to be hands-on rather than quantitative, so they can stay close to their customers. U.S. business can apply kaizen principles by concentrating on culture (company involvement in customer retention, listening, and leadership), information (customer segmentation, hands-on and formal research, and proactive complaint generation), and action (deployment and teamwork).

Chapter 12: Customer Retention and Its Role in Total Quality and the Continuous Improvement Process

To ensure continuous improvement—kaizen—and keep constant focus on customer retention, companies should apply a four-element voice of the customer (VOC) system that includes: planning (assessment of current state); gathering (identification of needs, expectations, problems, and complaints); understanding (collection and analysis of customer data); and deploying (use of the data to take appropriate action). Establishment of a customer information group or department within the company is one suggested approach to help manage the system and keep it effectively targeted at keeping customers.

As a final introductory note, some may question the book's subtitle, "An Integrated Process for Keeping Your Best Customers," with regard to using the word *best*. Companies dealing in reality should not want to keep all of their customers. Some customers are too small, some are too demanding, and some are too fickle and unreliable. Efficient concentration of effort and resources on the best customers, especially in retention activities, will help ensure the business's good health. Similar concentration in prospecting and acquisition will add only the most attractive customers to the company's list, in other words, those worth retaining.

Chapter 1

The Myth of Customer Satisfaction

An organization rarely finds its most valuable asset on the balance sheet. Yet this asset—customer satisfaction—has more impact on long-term performance than any other variable in business today.
—Introductory sentence from a customer
market research supplier's brochure

The ability of a company to satisfy customers may be its most important aftermarketing attribute.
—Terry G. Vavra, *Aftermarketing*

To satisfy the customer is the mission and purpose of every business.
—Peter Drucker

Examining the Myth

Companies generally think of customers in two ways: they *are* or they *are not*. While it is a convenient categorization, this yes-no perspective misses the reality of customer-provider relationships. There can, effectively, be up to five stages of a customer's life with any organization.

1. *Acquisition.* Winning the prospect; making the prospect a customer
2. *Retention.* Keeping the customer; obtaining the economic benefit of a long-term relationship
3. *Attrition.* Breaking down of loyalty; those performance attributes, customer-provider transactions, unmet expectations, and problems or complaints that can cause a customer to reduce or terminate purchases
4. *Defection.* Ending the relationship; the customer has gone to a competitor for products or services

5. *Reacquisition.* Getting the customer back; new initiatives or problem correction resulting in bringing the customer to the company again

There is general agreement that keeping customers loyal lowers costs and increases sales and profits.

> By far the largest costs that outstanding service saves are those of re-placing lost customers. There is no proven method for measuring these savings, but a common rule of thumb is that the marketing costs of landing a new customer run three to five times the marketing costs of retaining an old one . . . loyal customers offer their suppliers a triple payoff. They buy instead of being sold, so the marketing and sales costs of reaching them are lower than prospecting for new customers. Second, a company that deals with loyal customers knows a good deal about them and about how to get in touch with them, so the firm doesn't have to spend as much for transactions and communications—credit checking, or setting up new records for ordering, shipments and returns. And a very loyal customer buys more than the moderately loyal or new customer. In short, loyal customers are valuable not only because they represent lush streams of future revenues, but also because the costs of those revenues are small and the profits commensurately larger.[1] (Davidow and Uttal, *Total Customer Service*)

Companies can clearly benefit by increasing the lifetime spending of customers. Most companies, however, concentrate a highly dispro-portionate amount of their resources on attracting and acquiring customers, far less on keeping them. The conventional wisdom is that, once acquired, customers can be satisfied through superior products and services, and they will remain as customers.

This conventional wisdom, expanded to mythical levels in recent years, has a major drawback. Similar to the doctrine propounded by Napoleon in Orwell's *Animal Farm* that "some animals are more equal than others,"[2] expressions of "guaranteed satisfaction" and "highest quality" and "knock-your-socks-off service" now generate little regis-tration or interest among customers. It contributes in a one-dimension-al way, if at all, to a customer's relationship with a provider because many companies offer the same features. It has become just one more advertising or sales claim or slogan, even though many companies have raised the slogan to mission status.

Satisfied customers may be in either an attrition or defection process, and the unsuspecting company, focusing on satisfaction, will be totally unaware of these conditions. Writing in the Winter, 1995, is-sue of *Juran News*, Christopher Fry noted that, in a survey among 200 senior managers of US companies, the Juran Institute was almost completely unable to identify a bottom line improvement resulting from documented increases in customer satisfaction.[3] Frederick Reichheld of the consulting firm Bain & Co. has found that

> While it may seem intuitive that increasing customer satisfaction will increase retention and therefore profits, the facts are contrary. Between 65 percent and 85 percent of customers who defect say they were satisfied or very satisfied with their former supplier. In the auto industry, satisfaction scores average 85 percent to 95 percent, while repurchase rates average 40 percent.[4]

Likewise, Christopher Fay stated

> Why would it be that so many would continue to vigorously espouse and relentlessly pursue a metric—customer satisfaction—which is not at all clearly tied to profit improvement? It would seem that most managers assume satisfaction scores to be positively correlated with customer behavior, i.e., results. The tacit belief is that as a customer grades a supplier with an increasingly higher satisfaction score, so should that customer increase share of spending on that supplier, pay a price premium, refer new prospects, and so forth. In point of fact, this assumed correlation between what customers say and what they do has been disproved in the vast majority of businesses studied.[5]

Other findings are consistently similar to Reichheld's and Fay's. In one recent study, formerly frequent purchasing customers (who hadn't purchased anything in almost a year) gave satisfaction scores on service and product quality almost identical to active customers. This is shown in Table 1.1.

Clearly, the client involved in this study would have gotten little or no direction from these data if satisfaction were the principal or only basis for success or failure. If customers who had discontinued

Table 1.1. Excellent Quality Ratings.*

	Overall quality of service	Overall quality of products
Active buyers— 10–15+ purchases in past year	88%	79%
Inactive buyers— Formerly made 10–15+ purchases a year, but haven't purchased in last 8–10 months	84%	76%

*Five on a five-point scale of satisfaction

purchasing were as satisfied with the client's products and services as those still buying, there must have been other reasons for the defections. There were.

A close evaluation of customer needs, specific transactions, complaints, expectations, and perceptual gaps between the customers and service providers—all of which will be examined and discussed in detail in this book—revealed service, product, promotion, and communication performance attributes directly impacting customer retention.

Sometimes a company invests resources on improving weak customer satisfaction attributes, believing that fixing them will improve overall satisfaction. When that doesn't happen, they are left scratching their heads. In one case, attribute satisfaction scores went up and overall satisfaction went down. Similar results have been found in project after project, whether in consumer product, consumer service, or business-to-business product or service situations. Still, corporate America persists in its belief that customer satisfaction is the panacea for success.

> Customers are the reason (company name) exists, and if we satisfy our customers, we will increase our market share worldwide and that means superior financial returns. (President, major business products corporation)

> . . . when the service reaches the external customer, satisfaction is built in at every step and becomes 'permanent fixture'. (Senior executive, major service corporation)

> At (company name), customer satisfaction is the master plan. (Executive, auto manufacturer)

A sampling of brochures from industry customer satisfaction conferences has presentation titles like the following:

"Best Practices for Achieving Customer Satisfaction"

"Designing Business-to-Business Satisfaction Programs"

"Reengineering Support Functions to Optimize Customer Satisfaction"

"Maintaining a World-Class Customer Satisfaction Process"

"(Name) Corporation's Customer Satisfaction Process"

"Strategies for Achieving 100% Customer Satisfaction"

Bookstore business sections are crammed with ever-increasing numbers of how-to books on customer satisfaction, from auto dealers to supermarket retailers. The premise is that satisfaction is closely linked to quality, but is it?

Quality and Customer Satisfaction

Customer satisfaction has become generally accepted as a necessary ingredient in providing quality products and services. This is not just an observation and judgment, but a statement of fact supported in many books and articles on total quality management (TQM).

For example, here are some statements by leading authorities from academia and business.

> Industry accepts customer satisfaction as the goal of QFD [quality function deployment] because its advocates believe that, in the long-run, satisfied customers are an asset of the firm. Future short-run strategies can be adjusted to draw profitably on this asset.[6] (Abbie Griffin, University of Chicago, and John R. Hauser, MIT)

> High customer satisfaction is an indicator of perceived quality.[7] (Claes Fornell, University of Michigan)

> . . . the new philosophy is based on the knowledge that satisfied customers bring sales, and continuous improvement in customer satisfaction brings sales growth and increased market share. This in turn will not only generate higher profits, but will provide competitive strength for long-term business vitality and keep constant pressure on the competition. Therefore, the new service organization must develop a philosophy and culture based on the belief that customer satisfaction is the highest operational priority. (Total quality consultant)

> We will be the (listing of products) company providing products of SUPERIOR DESIGN and services that multiply value, with people dedicated to QUALITY and the TOTAL SATISFACTION of clients. (Vision statement of business products corporation)

> Customer satisfaction is the key to quality.[8] (Johnson A. Edosomwan, president and CEO, Johnson and Johnson Associates, Inc.)

> Position clear cut industry leadership in customer satisfaction within three years. (Long-term objective statement of business products corporation)

The Malcolm Baldrige National Quality Award, in fact, bases part of its point awarding process on the rate at which firms measure and generate increased levels of customer satisfaction. Category 7.0 includes assessments of company satisfaction research and analysis process and how the company compares in satisfaction levels to competitors.

Established in 1987, the Baldrige Award has become both a trailblazer and lightening rod for American business and helped legitimize the concept of customer satisfaction. Writing in a 1991 *Harvard Business Review* article, Professor David A. Garvin observed

The Baldrige Award not only codifies the principles of quality management in clear and accessible language. It also goes further: it provides companies with a comprehensive framework for assessing their progress toward the new paradigm of management and such commonly acknowledged goals as customer satisfaction and increased employee involvement.[9]

Although customer satisfaction is a stated goal of the Baldrige Award, there is contradictory, even negative, evidence of winners' competitiveness. For example, in May 1990, the General Accounting Office (GAO) published "Management Practices—U.S. Companies Improve Performance Through Quality Efforts," a report detailing the quality programs of 20 companies that had scored high in the 1988 and 1989 award.[10] Among key results, reporting companies indicated that, while customer satisfaction levels had increased among these companies, customer retention levels had remained almost unchanged (see Table 1.2).

The Cadillac division of General Motors, for instance, won the Baldrige Award in 1990. Since then, however, its sales results have been less than impressive. Further, quality evaluation sources such as *Consumer Reports* and J. D. Power have not rated them higher. (It should be noted, however, that the J. D. Power Customer Satisfaction Index is not directly tied to future purchase likelihood, so there is every possibility that the ratings could have been higher with little or no effect on sales.)

Responding to David Garvin's article, the debate over the Baldrige Award, its relevancy and gauge of customer-related corporate performance (incorporating customer satisfaction) continues.

Table 1.2. Selected Results from the GAO Study.

Customer satisfaction indicators	Number of responding companies	Directions of Indicator			Average annual improvement
		Positive (favorable)	Negative (unfavorable)	No change	
Overall customer satisfaction	14	12	0	2	2.5%
Customer retention	10	4	2	4	1.0%

Source: "Management Practices—U.S. Companies Improve Performance Through Quality Efforts," Washington, D.C.: General Accounting Office, May 1990 (GAO NSIAD91-190).

Companies that wish to compete for the award must produce evidence of leadership and long-term planning, initiate verifiable quality control procedures, address the happiness and well-being of the work force, and above all, work toward the satisfaction of the customer.[11] (Arden G. Sims, president and CEO, Globe Metallurgical Inc.)

. . . the Baldrige is a quality award, not a business excellence award. Including financial results would shift the chances of winning away from those applicants who have effective quality processes and weak financial results. It would create the false impression that high quality and good financial results are much more closely linked than they are in practice.[12] (Bradley T. Gale, founder, Market Driven Quality, Inc.)

Many stalled TQM programs share a lack of results orientation, a criticism that the Baldrige Award is also subject to. . . . All too often, correlation with results is not important and not to be looked for.[13] (Phil Fifer, principal, McKinsey & Company)

An award of this status can't afford not to put some emphasis on profitability. Achieving superior quality is not the destination that businesses strive for, profitability is. The quality process must be part of the road map to financial results along with market strategy, research and development, and so on. After all, businesses are rewarded in the real world for results.[14] (Gail E. Cooper, chairman of the board, Cooper Consulting Co., Inc.)

One of the more interesting link-ups between customer satisfaction and TQM has been achieved by Dr. Noriaki Kano. Kano is professor at the Science University of Tokyo and an international consultant and lecturer in quality management, marketing, and statistics. He is perhaps best recognized as the advocate of "attractive quality vs. must-be quality," also known as the Kano model.

Rather than follow the traditional one-dimensional perspective on customer satisfaction, that is, that the better a company does at delivering on each service attribute, the more satisfied their customers will be, Kano's model suggests that there are three types of performance, or quality, attributes.

1. Exciting, surprising, attractive performance, which increases customer satisfaction if completed; no effect if not completed.

2. Desired, or one-dimensional performance, which has no effect on customer satisfaction; is neither positive nor negative.

3. Expected, or must be performance, which decreases customer satisfaction if not completely performed.

Customer satisfaction

Very satisfied

ATTRACTIVE

ONE-DIMENSIONAL

Degree of **Did not**   **Fully**
achievement **do at all**   **achieved**

EXPECTED

Very dissatisfied

Source: Nariaki Kano, Nobuhiro Seraku, Fumio Takahashi, Shinichi Tsuji, "Attractive Quality and Must Be Quality," *Quality* 14, no. 2 (1984): 39–48.

Figure 1.1. The Kano model.

He also views achievement, the delivery of a service performance attribute, as a key dimension. The Kano model is shown in Figure 1.1.

Achievement on some attributes will increase customer satisfaction, but after a certain point, increasing achievement will no longer contribute to satisfaction. These are *expected attributes*—failure to deliver on these will result in dissatisfaction. An auto lubrication service, for example, changes oil and oil filters, normally in 15 minutes, for $15.95. If it puts in poor quality oil (or the wrong grade), installs an inferior oil filter, takes 30 minutes for the service, or overcharges the customer, one or more of these could create dissatisfaction, says Kano, in some cases strong dissatisfaction.

Some attributes follow the traditional perspective described. There is a linear relation between attribute achievement and customer satisfaction. These *desired*, or *one-dimensioned attributes* (for example, price) are typically the basis for competition between various service providers. Applying the lubrication service example, if the service uses standard quality oil or filters, charges $15.95, and completes the service in 15 minutes, these will result in neither increased or decreased satisfaction because all competitors offer these products and services.

The final type of attribute is termed *surprising* or *attractive*. Nonachievement on these attributes will not diminish customer satisfaction, but as a company begins to deliver these features, customer satisfaction can accelerate. Top brands of oil or filters, price specials or coupons, 10 minute service—these may increase satisfaction according to Kano.

Kano, reflective of the prevailing views of American business, quality consultants, and academics, has recently defined his philosophy behind TQM, again incorporating the concept of satisfaction.

> Total Quality Management is business management which is exercised under the philosophy that the best way for a corporation to expand sales and make a profit is to provide its customers with satisfaction through its products and services.

To illustrate his philosophy and model, he has used the opening paragraph of the Heike Tale, the famous Japanese story of the rise and fall of the Heike family, which governed Japan as the emperor's surrogate during Japan's feudal period.[15]

> All things flow and nothing is permanent.
> The color of cherry tree flowers:
>   it expresses the reason
>   the prosperous must inevitably decline
> A person who lives even in luxury cannot survive so long:
>   it is just something like a dream at spring night
> A fearless man perishes someday:
>   It is the same with dust before a wind blows.

While instructive (even poetic), Kano's take on the value of customer satisfaction is that if dissatisfied by certain areas or attributes, the customer inevitably will do something like slow or stop purchasing, that is, cease to exist as a productive customer. As we have found, however, the customer, though satisfied or dissatisfied, may also do nothing, that is, remain as an active customer.

Perhaps the most ringing endorsement toward customer retention and away from a satisfaction focus has come from the late international quality expert, Dr. W. Edwards Deming. In *Out of the Crisis*, he said,

> It will not suffice to have customers that are merely satisfied. An unhappy customer will switch. Unfortunately, a satisfied customer may also switch, on the theory that he could not lose much, and might gain. Profit in business comes from repeat customers, customers that boast about your product and service, and that bring friends with them. Fully allocated costs may well show that the profit in a transaction with a customer that comes back voluntarily may be 10 times the profit realized from a customer that responds to advertising and other persuasion.[16]

The myth of customer satisfaction, then, is the leap of faith and orientation of business that satisfaction equals action, and that a company, if it is satisfying customers, can consider itself on safe ground. We begin to examine this myth and offer dynamic approaches to understanding and keeping customers in the next chapter.

Summary

Conventional wisdom of business, academia, and the consulting community is that customer satisfaction is a necessary element and cornerstone of total quality, and that, if satisfied, the customer will remain loyal. This is the myth, and potential drawback, of having a total customer satisfaction focus. Reality proves that customer loyalty or retention is a more complex, yet more definitive, indicator of quality performance.

Notes

1. William H. Davidow and Bro Uttal, *Total Customer Service: The Ultimate Weapon* (New York: Harper & Row, 1989), 30.

2. George Orwell, *Animal Farm* (New York: Alfred A. Knopf, 1993), 88.

3. Christopher J. Fay, "Can't Get No Satisfaction? Perhaps You Should Stop Trying," *Juran News* (Winter 1995):1.

4. Frederick F. Reichheld, "Loyalty-Based Management," *Harvard Business Review* (March–April 1993): 71.

5. Fay, "Can't Get No Satisfaction? Perhaps You Should Stop Trying," 1.

6. Abbie Griffin and John R. Hauser, "The Voice of the Customer," *Marketing Science* 12 (Winter 1993): 20.

7. Claes Fornell, "A National Customer Satisfaction Index," presentation to AMA/ASQC Third Annual Customer Satisfaction and Quality Measurement Conference, Washington, D. C., April 1991.

8. Johnson A. Edosomwan, "Implementing Customer-Driven Quality Improvement Projects," *The Quality Observer* (November 1991): 5.

9. David A. Garvin, "How the Baldrige Award Really Works," *Harvard Business Review* (November–December 1991): 80.

10. "Management Practices—U.S. Companies Improve Performance Through Quality Efforts," Washington, D.C.: General Accounting Office (May 1990), GAO NSIAD 91–190.

11. "Does the Baldrige Award Really Work?" *Harvard Business Review* (January–February 1992): 126.

12. Ibid., 132.

13. Ibid., 138.

14. Ibid., 139.

15. Helen Craig McCullough (trans.), *The Tale of the Heike* (Stanford, Calif.: Stanford University Press, 1988), 51.

16. W. Edwards Deming, *Out of the Crisis* (Cambridge, Mass.: Massachusetts Institute of Technology, 1982), 141.

Chapter 2

Customer Satisfaction vs. Customer Retention

A good carpenter will not throw wood away. A good general will not discard a warrior. A nine-story tower begins with the foundation.[1]
— Takeda Nobushige (1525–1561 A.D.)

Success is getting the right customers—and keeping them.[2]
— MBNA Annual Report, 1991

The purpose of business is to get and keep customers.[3]
— Theodore Levitt

Why Retention Is a Different . . . and Better . . . Indicator of Quality Performance

Companies focused on optimizing customer retention, as opposed to satisfaction, may be challenged to explain why retention or loyalty is truly a different and more effective mind-set and not just an alternative spin on customer satisfaction. A quick check with the nearest *Webster's Dictionary* will show striking differences between the words *satisfy* or *satisfaction* and *retain* or *retention*.

Satisfy: To make content or appease, to fulfill requirements

Retain: To keep or use, or to hold or continue to hold in possession.[4]

Retention is clearly the more action-oriented of these two words. Yet most customer service management and customer service measurement, no matter how comprehensive, is constructed around achieving the highest levels of satisfaction, not retention.

In some industries, customer satisfaction scores tend to correlate with retention. In other industries, there is little or no correlation. Overriding the issue of correlation is the issue of value, flexibility and utility as a keystone customer service quality measurement device. Is satisfaction or retention the more reliable measure?

As demonstrated, studies in many industries have proven that it is entirely possible to (1) understand customer demanded wants and needs; (2) measure satisfaction levels of current customers, former customers, and competitors' customers; (3) assess employees' roles in the satisfaction process; and (4) have high customer satisfaction levels—and still be losing customers. Customers, who, through direct company contact or surveys, say they're satisfied today, can defect next week, next month, or next year.

In *Aftermarketing*, Terry Vavra states, "Numerous studies show that repurchase likelihood is directly related to satisfaction rating,"[5] and goes on to show in an exhibit that there is "strong direct correlation" (see Figure 2.1), but doesn't explain the data.

Where there is a positive sales and service experience, repurchase likelihood is high—there is very strong correlation with satisfaction. And even when the sales or service experience has been negative, there is still strong correlation between satisfaction and repurchase likelihood. So when customers defect, they will be highly satisfied; and, if using satisfaction scores as the definitive measure, a company won't know why these customers left.

In the scatter diagram of Figure 2.1, there is also moderate to high positive correlation between product satisfaction and likelihood to repurchase. Note, however, that there are several instances in which there was 90 percent or better complete product satisfaction coupled with 60 percent or less intention to repurchase. Also, there were several cases in which there was under 10 percent product satisfaction coupled with 40 percent or higher repurchase intent. These results hardly represent definitive direction.

The bottom line is that, at a minimum, satisfaction is a somewhat unreliable indicator of customer loyalty. At worst, it can be completely unreliable. A balanced view is that as a sole predictor, or basis of evaluating performance, it must be regarded as inconsistent and suspect. Attrition factors are much more directional than satisfaction scores alone.

The Concept and Value
of an Attrition Focus

Attrition has several definitions, but the most generally accepted is "gradual wearing down or grinding down." As applied to customers,

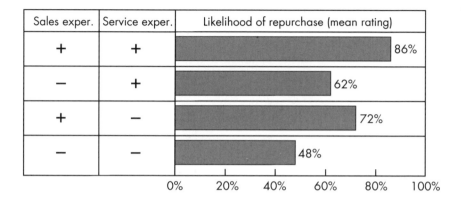

Sales exper.	Service exper.	Likelihood of repurchase (mean rating)
+	+	86%
−	+	62%
+	−	72%
−	−	48%

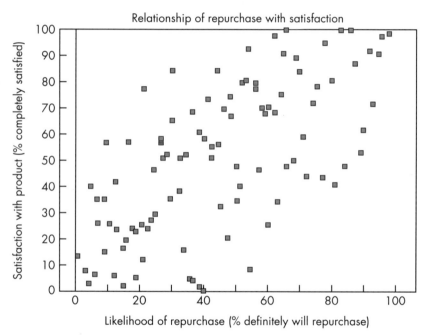

Figure caption area (scatter plot): Relationship of repurchase with satisfaction

Y-axis: Satisfaction with product (% completely satisfied)
X-axis: Likelihood of repurchase (% definitely will repurchase)

Source: Reprinted with permission from Terry G. Vavra, *Aftermarketing.* (Homewood, Ill.: Richard D. Irwin, 1992), 168.

Figure 2.1. The relationship between satisfaction and repurchase.

it is that state in which a customer, for personal reasons, begins to question continued patronage of a supplier.

There can be one or many reasons contributing to attrition, and they can each have different degrees of impact. For the supplier interested in retaining customers, identifying and acting upon these reasons, in the order of their priority, will frequently mark the difference between success and failure.

Attrition factors can be major, or they can be small and insidious. Business to business, industry to industry, there are few common denominators. For a new car dealer, it can be poor after-sale customer follow-up; for an industrial products company, it may be occasional stock shortages by some suppliers; for a commercial bank, it may be the lack of Saturday hours.

In *In Search of Excellence*, Peters and Waterman's number one principal is to have a bias for action, and number two is staying close to the customer.[6] They also advise locating and eliminating small problems before they become big. Seeking out attrition factors effectively combines these two principles in a highly focused manner.

Perhaps the best direction on identifying attrition factors comes from a sixteenth century Japanese swordmaster, Miyamoto Musashi. In his instructional text, *The Book of Five Rings,* Musashi identified nine precepts that he felt would bring success in life. Three of these apply to attrition.

- "Nurture the ability to perceive the truth in all matters." That is, develop intuitive judgement and understanding.
- "Perceive that which cannot be seen with the eye."
- "Do not be negligent, even in trifling matters."[7]

Musashi followed the samurai idea of *kan-ken,* or two eyesights. The first is the cultivation of diligence and the second is keen intuition. In the last of these precepts, Musashi has given meaning to the ancient samurai saying, "from one comes many." Loosely translated, this represents the small things that, taken together, can equal success or failure. With regard to customers, this can be a seemingly minor service delivery or product reaction, a concern or complaint, or a series of them. And, although the customer appears satisfied or even claims to be satisfied, he or she is actually on the way out the door.

So, the operative approach to minimizing or eliminating customer attrition is *proaction.* Watch the door. This will be reemphasized throughout the book.

Talking to Former Customers and Intermediate Customers

When a customer becomes angry enough, frustrated enough, or tired enough of poor product or service performance, defection is often the outcome. And, within that outcome, more often than not there will be little input from the former customer as to why that decision was made.

Many companies dismiss former customers as lost causes, particularly in good times when the business is growing and new customers are rapidly being added. They believe that debriefing them will add little value within the mission of satisfying current customers. This is a very narrow perspective. Feedback from former customers is almost as important as customers in an attrition mode. It often mirrors or intensifies the reasons for customer attrition. As stated by Reichheld and Sasser, "Customers who leave can provide a view of the business that is unavailable on the inside. And whatever caused one individual to defect may cause many others to follow. The idea is to use defections as an early warning signal—to learn from defectors why they left the company, and to use that information to improve the business."[8]

If a fast food company offers customers high prices, slow service, cold food, dirty stores, and surly personnel, and fails to debrief the customers who have become disappointed and left, it is theoretically possible to reinforce and perpetuate this negative product and service performance because those few customer remaining say they are satisfied.

From former customers, companies can identify

- What quality of products or services competitors offer
- Concerns and complaints, whether expressed or unexpressed, leading to defection
- Assessment of former suppliers' product and service performance
- Likelihood of repurchase from former supplier

With this information in hand, companies are better able to identify and prioritize areas of product or service challenge and to assess the degree of effort needed in trying to reacquire former customers. Former customer feedback interpretation will be treated more fully in a later chapter.

Intermediate customers, such as retailers, distributors, and manufacturers' representatives, are the people who interface with both the product/service provider and the end users. They can offer insight into the quality of delivery to end users, especially when a supplier doesn't deal directly with end customers. Their value as an information source will also be covered in greater detail later in the book.

An Example of Satisfaction Focus Disadvantage—Complaints

Relying heavily on an extensive, but reactive, complaint handling system (such as 800 lines) to monitor customer satisfaction would be highly inappropriate, even misleading. Several years ago, Cynthia Grimm identified several problems with using complaint data in this regard. To paraphrase her findings

- Many customers don't make the effort to complain; however, these customers often defect.
- Complaining customers may have demographic and personality profiles different from other buyers.
- Registered complaints may not be representative of customer problems.
- Registered complaints don't suggest the extent of dissatisfaction.[9]

Perhaps the most telling deficiency with reactive complaint data is this: Up to 90 percent of complaints are never registered,[10] yet it is frequently the unregistered complaints that have the greatest impact on customer retention. In other words, a company can have high satisfaction scores and an excellent and sensitive complaint monitoring system and can still be losing their best, most profitable customers due to (1) inadequate methods of generating unregistered complaints and (2) no effort to relate all (registered and unregistered) complaints to retention.

Companies must do more than respond to expressed customer complaints. Since customers won't, in many cases, express complaints, even with elaborate prompting and handling systems, truly customer-driven companies will simply ask customers (including former customers) for unregistered complaints and ask why they weren't registered. They must lead the customer; be ahead of competitors; and anticipate wants, needs, and concerns. They must establish a relationship between registered complaints, unregistered complaints, and customer attrition and defection.

According to A. Beeler Gausz, president of the Quality College, service quality reaction is kinetic, often instant. In settings where any breakdown in service, however seemingly small and insignificant, can cause attrition or defection, companies must take a proactive position on performance and complaints.

It's search and seizure—the customers search for the least disappointing service, and the suppliers seize each others' disappointed customers. Service customers themselves are important sources of requirements for quality service. But remember, they don't ordinarily say much unless the service needs improvement, and then it's too late.[11]

How a Retention Approach to Customer Complaints Helped Turn the Situation Around

A major regional discount hardware and lumber chain had, for several years, monitored key performance attributes, but relied on customer service desks in each store to keep appraised of problems and complaints. It kept track of registered complaints on a fairly detailed basis: by store, area, region, and total system. However, it was losing customers at a rapid pace in several regions where a competitor had recently upgraded its store interiors, pricing, brand selection, and service. As the chain was receiving high performance satisfaction scores, even while customers were defecting, management recognized that the customer service research system was not helping to retain customers or address improvement issues.

The company's first task was to develop a full list, or inventory, of customer complaints. Of course, it was already monitoring registered complaints at the store level, but it had no idea if this was representative of all customer complaints.

As part of the customer service research redirection process, personal in-depth interviews, minigroups, and full focus groups were conducted with former customers, current customers, and store employees (managers and service staff). In addition to learning about service attributes, customer-provider transactions, and performance expectations, a complete listing of complaints, both registered and unregistered, was developed. Among the new things learned were

- Customer service representatives were not empowered to make adjustments or replacements above a certain dollar amount.
- Floor service personnel had inconsistent depth of knowledge regarding lumber and hardware.
- There were too few floor service personnel available, and customers often had to wait up to 15 minutes to have a product or usage question handled.
- Checkout was often slow, with most registers handling checks, cash, and credit, and customer lines were occasionally six deep.

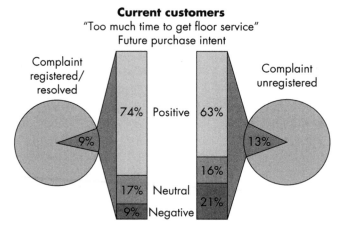

Current customers
"Too much time to get floor service"
Future purchase intent

Source: ARBOR, Inc., 1991.

Figure 2.2. Current customers' complaints.

When proactive complaint monitoring was added to the customer research process, it was found that 9 percent of current customers had registered "too much time to get floor service" (Figure 2.2).[12] In most cases, this complaint issue had been resolved, but it still caused 26 percent of those who had registered the complaint to be neutral or negative about future purchase intent (though many had also given positive overall satisfaction ratings to the chain).

Serious as the floor service timing issue was among those customers who had registered this complaint, the impact of service timing as an unregistered complaint was dramatically greater. Over 13 percent of current customers had not registered floor service timing as a complaint until asked in the research. This was almost half again as high as the proportion of customers who had complained. The effect on customer retention was also substantially higher. Almost 37 percent of the customers who had not registered this complaint were neutral to negative about their future purchase intentions, compared to 26 percent who had registered the complaint.

The most damaging effect of waiting for complaints to happen and then reacting to them can be seen in the measurements of floor service timing complaints among former customers (Figure 2.3). Almost 15 percent of the former customers identified floor service timing as a registered complaint, and though resolved, this issue was serious enough that 42 percent of those customers were neutral or negative about purchasing again. That set of figures got the chain's attention, but what really proved the value of a proactive retention focus was the

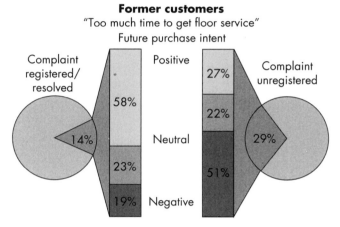

Former customers
"Too much time to get floor service"
Future purchase intent

Source: ARBOR, Inc., 1991.

Figure 2.3. Former customers' complaints.

effect of slow floor service among former customers who had not complained about it. Close to 30 percent had not complained, and, of that group, almost three quarters were neutral or negative about purchasing at the chain again.[13]

Slow, unresponsive floor service time was clearly a complaint area requiring priority and major surgery by the chain. The incidence of registered floor service complaints and problems was no higher than other service issues, and yet once its severity was identified as an unregistered complaint, it became the first area for quality improvement focus.

Are Registered Complaints and Patient Satisfaction a Cure-All for Health Care?

A large regional hospital consortium was concerned enough about the impact of patient (customer) complaints that it regularly had key management staff monitor complaint and service telephones. Certainly a very positive effort in generating voice of the customer, but, again, not effective enough in getting to patient loyalty.

Any health care service measurement system, whether inpatient our outpatient, is complex. There is a great deal of dependence on close, interpersonal relationships between caregivers and patients. That said, it is nevertheless important to have both registered and unregistered complaints. Just as in other customer-provider situations, they will have a profound effect on loyalty.

Adding to the complexity of health service measurement are the various aspects of care.

- Medical staff—Staff capability and sensitivity
- Medical facilities—Testing, rehabilitation, and so on
- Housekeeping—Room cleanliness and comfort, food quality and variety, equipment/facilities availability and quality, noise levels, and so on
- Support—Admissions/discharge procedures, food service facilities, support staff courtesy/speed, volunteer participation, parking, and shops

As in other industries, complaint data in health care, to the extent that they are generated and analyzed, are usually correlated to overall performance or satisfaction ratings, not loyalty. While performance items like food quality and noise levels tend to not correlate highly with overall satisfaction, they do with loyalty. In addition, just as in retail sales, many of these health care housekeeping and support services tend to generate more unregistered complaints, which lead to patient disloyalty.

In health care, because so much of the service is high touch, closely related to patients' health, safety, and physical and mental well-being, *all* complaints, both those registered with doctors, nurses, or support staff, and, particularly, those not registered, must be gathered. The hospital consortium in this example began complaint generation by having staffers call recently released patients to identify specific complaints as well as overall performance. They uncovered an emerging dimension of latent dissatisfaction: *time,* which transcended many areas of hospital service.

This dimension included seemingly unrelated contact points between customer and provider.

- Responsiveness of doctors and nurses to patient requests and time spent with them
- Reliability of meal delivery, meal clearing, and services such as television installation
- Waiting time for X-rays and tests
- Admissions efficiency

A proactive approach was taken with latent complaints. It was added to the consortium's patient service survey process, and the complete spectrum of complaints were correlated with patient loyalty measures. This resulted in action being taken regarding responsiveness, and housekeeping/support staff efficiency, and both overall patient satisfaction and loyalty increased.

The effect of complaints will be more fully examined in a later chapter.

An Exercise to Build On

There will be only one exercise used in this book. It will represent customer service and measurement situations occurring across many industries. Each succeeding chapter will offer skills and direction designed to improve retention focus and quality management techniques, and the exercise will provide opportunity to apply what has been presented in that chapter.

As the senior customer service and total quality officer of Twentieth Century National (a 50-branch, major regional bank), you have been measuring customer satisfaction for over ten years. Your customer satisfaction scores have shown steady improvement in all regions and for the entire banking system, yet you are now losing customers in two of the regions faster than you are generating new ones.

Bank management is concerned about the loss of revenue and deposits, and you are charged to help turn this situation around and soon. Begin thinking about an action plan based on retention measurement, rather than satisfaction.

Summary

Retention is a far more dynamic measure of customer service performance quality than satisfaction. Customers can give high satisfaction scores and then defect.

Understanding attrition, the reasons customers' loyalty diminishes, is an essential consideration to help determine why current customers may become disloyal. To better understand attrition factors, talk to former customers and intermediate customers such as retailers.

Correlating expressed complaints with satisfaction provides little direction for service quality improvement. Use both latent and registered complaints and correlate them with retention scores.

Notes

1. *Ideals of the Samurai,* William Scott Wilson trans. (Burbank, Calif.: Ohara Publications, 1982), 106.

2. MBNA Corporation, Newark, Del., 1991.

3. Theodore Levitt, *The Marketing Imagination* (New York: The Free Press, 1983).

4. *Webster's Third New International Dictionary,* 8th ed., s.v. "satisfy," "retain."

5. Terry G. Vavra, *Aftermarketing* (Homewood, Ill.: Business One Irwin, 1992), 167.

6. Thomas J. Peters and Robert H. Waterman, Jr., *In Search of Excellence* (New York: Warner Books, 1982), 13–14, 119–99.

7. Miyamoto Musashi, *The Book of Five Rings (Gorin No Sho)* (New York Bantam Books, 1982), 24.

8. Frederick F. Feichheld and W. Earl Sasser, Jr., "Zero Defections: Quality Comes to Services," *Harvard Business Review* (September–October, 1990): 109.

9. Cyntha Grimm, "Understanding and Reading the Customer: Summary of Recent Research," *MOBIUS* 6 (1987): 14–19.

10. Based on ARBOR customer service research studies and corroborating data from several other sources and authors.

11. A. Beeler Gausz, "When Service Is Your Product, How Important Is Quality Management?" *Quality Update* (January–February 1992): 37–38.

12. Based on ARBOR customer service research study.

13. Based on ARBOR customer service research study.

The Six Failures and Five Cures of Customer Product and Service Performance Measurement

Many companies either do not include market-action questions in their measurement or they ask the wrong questions.[1]
—John A. Goodman, Scott M. Broetzmann, and Colin Adamson, in *Quality Progress*, May 1992

A man with deep far-sightedness will survey both the beginning and the end of a situation and continually consider its every facet as important.[2]
—General Takeda Shingen, *The Iwamizudera Monogatari*, (1521–1573)

The Six Failures

This chapter has been developed to be for the reader what a good point guard is for a basketball team: It will set up the principal subject to be covered in the remainder of the book.

A heightened awareness of customer fickleness and increased competition in virtually every industry has propelled many companies into the arena of customer service measurement. For the majority of them, this is both a relatively new and somewhat challenging process. Because they believe their focus should be on customer satisfaction, the measurement programs they institute will often give little or no direction on what it takes to keep customers.

There are six ways that most measurement programs can fail a company. It is eminently possible that a program will fail in more than one and may even fail in all. The six failures are measurement programs that

1. Follow rather than lead customers
2. Consider only registered complaints and ignore latent ones

3. Measure only global attributes, not operational elements

4. Ignore customer expectations

5. Ignore customer-provider gaps

6. Have a measurement goal of satisfaction, not loyalty or attrition

Let's examine them in detail.

1. Follow Rather Than Lead Customers

Most measurement systems are report cards, totally quantitative in nature, and treat only current customer needs. Often, it is the company—not the customer—that had identified many or all of the needs, with the customer having little or no opportunity to take the provider in appropriate new directions.

This is frequently how-are-we-doing? research that uses customer comment cards or superficial mail research and deals with tactical, Band-aid, quick fix type of answers rather than product or service strategy. Examples can be seen in Figure 3.1.

Restaurant Management Company

Dear Guests,
In the interest of maintaining and improving our high standards
of food quality and service, we would appreciate your comments
and suggestions. Please fill in this card and drop in any mailbox.
                    Thank you.

Restaurant location: _____

Date: _____   Time: _____

Drive-thru [   ]   Lobby [   ]   Lunch [   ]   Dinner [   ]

Items ordered: _____

How often do you visit? _____

Please check the box below that best applies.

	excellent	good	fair	poor	very poor
Food quality	☐	☐	☐	☐	☐
Speed of service	☐	☐	☐	☐	☐
Hospitality	☐	☐	☐	☐	☐
Order accuracy	☐	☐	☐	☐	☐
Cleanliness	☐	☐	☐	☐	☐

Name: _____

Address: _____

City: _____ State: _____ Zip: _____

Telephone number: (   ) _____

Comments . . .

Figure 3.1. Comment card examples.

How Are We Doing?
Please give your store a report card grade on each dimension.
A = Outstanding, F = Failing
(Circle letter)

	Grade
1. Having friendly employees..............	A B C D F
2. Finding help on the selling floor.......	A B C D F
3. Having employees who can usually answer my questions	A B C D F
4. Speed of checkout	A B C D F
5. Ease in returning/exchanging merchandise	A B C D F
6. Aisles are wide enough for easy shopping	A B C D F
7. Clothing is displayed on racks in a way that makes it easy to browse, see what's there	A B C D F
8. Being a neat and clean place to shop..	A B C D F
9. Having a good variety of merchandise	A B C D F
10. Carrying wanted name brands	A B C D F
11. Offering low prices every day..........	A B C D F
12. Having new, fresh merchandise	A B C D F
13. Having good quality merchandise....	A B C D F
14. Usually find what I'm looking for	A B C D F
15. As an overall place to shop	A B C D F

OPTIONAL:

NAME _____

STREET _____

CITY _____ STATE_____ ZIP _____

PHONE ( )_____

☐ I would like a reply   ☐ I don't need a reply

Questions or Additional Comments . . .
Call Toll Free
1-800-XXX-XXXX

Source: Examples of comment cards from M. Lowenstein's file of over 200.

Figure 3.1. *(continued)*

Seeing low-rated attributes, companies rush to plug up or cement over these areas by investing or diverting resources to meet them. Scores on these attributes, however, give no indication of either importance to the customer or the impact on his or her potential for continued purchase, and so offer the company no leverage. As a result, these resources can be wasted or, at minimum, utilized inefficiently.

As consultant Frederick F. Reichheld has said, "Companies that fail to use their knowledge of customers to develop the product or service those customers will need next are leaving the door open for another company to lure them away."[3] Customer needs have only one element of constancy—they are constantly changing. To remain competitive, companies have little choice but to know where customer needs are trending.

2. Consider Only Registered Complaints and Ignore Latent Ones

Companies can develop elaborate systems to capture customer complaints—24-hour toll free service lines and the like. This extends to the customer satisfaction research instruments they use to learn more about customers.

What companies fail to recognize is that very few customers—as few as 5 percent who have complaints—actually ever formally register them. Many of the rest do not express them because of time, fear of confrontation, and so on. As a result, companies cannot generate a reliable model for improvement based only on expressed complaints. Additionally, we often find that unexpressed complaints are the more serious issues that can create greater customer attrition and departure. Denis Walker has warned, "Relying on unsolicited customer comment is rarely sufficient to give a good picture of customer views. It is in every service organization's interest to elicit as much customer comment as possible. Few companies have a systematic way of doing this."[4]

For example, a publishing client first debriefed customer service supervisory staff on what customers were saying before going out to identify customers' real needs, expectations, problems, and complaints. The qualitative customer information gathered was then converted into attributes and other performance measures in the quantitative research. The findings, reflective of so many other projects, were that the methods to hear customer complaints produced findings very different from what the company's customer service staff was hearing. Service staff tends to receive only the most negative feedback, sometimes punctuated with customer emotion. Proactive complaint generation provides a full cross-sectional complaint inventory that can then be examined for retention impact.

Some companies also believe that low attribute performance ratings in their surveys are analogous to complaints. This simply is incorrect. Low attribute ratings may represent problem areas right enough, but a complaint is performance poor enough and important enough that a customer would consider making an issue of it. Complaint identification and inventorying is vital to a customer retention focus.

3. Measure Only Global Attributes, Not Operational Elements

Many companies, as illustrated in Figure 3.1, ask for customer feedback on the broadest of performance attributes, believing, to paraphrase Total Quality experts, that "it can't be managed if it isn't measured." Often attributes are so global, or operationally vague, they are inactionable.

Every time a customer comes in contact with a company's products or services, there may be scores of individual deliveries or transactions involved. Businesses with high levels of customer interaction—lodging, banking, investment services, travel, and health care, to name a few—will also have high transaction levels.

Since the goal of any measurement program is true actionability and performance improvement, it may be more important to look at these operational elements than attributes. For example, the fast food restaurant comment card in Figure 3.1 measures several dimensions of performance, including food quality, hospitality, and cleanliness. Does *food quality* mean that hot food was served hot and cold food cold, the food was fresh, the food tasted good, and so on? Does *hospitality* mean how the customer was greeted, how the order was taken, how the food was delivered, and so on? Does *cleanliness* mean inside or outside of the restaurant, the floors, table and counter areas, the food trays, the bathrooms, the service staff's clothing, and so on?

In customer research projects conducted for auto dealerships, *service time* can have up to 15 separate components. Like the fast food restaurant example, they all deserve measurement, since any could contribute to customer attrition or loss.

4. Ignore Customer Expectations

It can rightly be said that customer expectations are a moving target. Change is constant due to the players: the economy, competition, and consumer need. Customers can be influenced by evolutionary market and product situations, such as higher speed and capacity personal computers, and attachments contributing to versatility, such as CD-rom.

Expectations may change as buyers come into a market. Initial buyers of a product or service may be more adventurous and less demanding. As more customers move into the market, they may want performance guarantees, pricing concessions, or other assurances of value. Companies should account for this in their measurement systems.

Expectations must be identified every time measurement is performed. Otherwise, providers risk not knowing how much (or how little) of a performance attribute to offer. In *Delivering Quality Service*, Zeithaml, Parasuraman, and Berry state that "Service quality, as perceived by customers, can be defined as the extent of discrepancy between customers' expectations or desires and their perceptions."[5] They identify several factors that can contribute to customers' expectations.

- What customers hear from other customers. If a friend or acquaintance recommends a product or service, it is expected that performance will be at least to the level described.

- Personal needs of customers can govern expectations. A busy executive may expect quick service at a lunch meal, while a retired customer, with fewer time demands, has lesser expectations of service.

- Customers' past experiences with a product or service contribute to expectations. Customers of a shoe repair shop might expect three day turn-around to have shoes resoled because it has taken that amount of time for years.

- Communication from the product or service provider creates a level of expectation. Furniture store ads boasting "the largest selection in town," fancy hotel brochures describing their accommodations and facilities, and fertilizer packages guaranteeing a "greener lawn in 30 days," are some of the ways advertising can create expectations.[6]

Rather than first explore the boundaries of customer expectation and then include them in the measurement system, too often companies either presume they know what customers expect or else choose to ignore expectations altogether. Either course is dangerous.

5. Ignore Customer-Provider Gaps

If customers tell a company (through its measurement program) that products and services are performing poorly, and that these areas of poor performance are important and may impact on their loyalty, shouldn't the company believe the results and take corrective action?

While an affirmative response would appear to be obvious, management and staff may be disinclined to act. Just as they sometimes do when considering customer expectations, they may feel that their years of experience or in-depth knowledge have anointed them with customer need sensitivity and insight.

Whether defined as culture, mind-set, or whatever, companies in denial, with an it-doesn't-happen-here attitude toward negative customer feedback, are challenged to make material change. This is not done overnight. It requires discipline, tracking, a kaizen, or continuous improvement, focus, and close ties to the customer.

In addition to using appropriate customer-research techniques, making research an ongoing activity, and deploying research through staff training, companies often never stop to realize that they can help close or eliminate customer-provider perceptual gaps by including staff in the research process.

Seeking staff involvement and input is not only positive from a company culture standpoint, it offers two other real advantages.

- Staff, particularly customer-facing staff like sales personnel and customer service representatives, can provide valuable insights into customer perceptions.

- Comparing staff responses to those provided by customers provides a believable, supportable platform for product or service improvement programs. It is difficult for management or frontline staff to conclude "it doesn't happen here" when their own results don't align with customers. More simply stated, formal staff input converts to an excellent deployment training device.

To further facilitate change, customer studies should have staff complete the same questionnaires or interviews given to customers. They should be instructed to answer as they believe customers would. Whether they see themselves performing better, worse, or similar to customers' perceptions, it is the comparisons, or areas of gap and alignment, that are most motivating to staff in a training for improvement setting. Some companies fail to recognize the benefits of this, but there is no downside to including staff.

6. Have a Measurement Goal of Satisfaction, Not Loyalty or Attrition

Many companies sincerely want to improve performance. That's why they set up measurement systems in the first place. Either through the stubborn acceptance of long-held conventional wisdom or lack of awareness or consideration of newer, more directional measures of performance, however, they continue to make customer satisfaction their goal, both through measurement and as a company imperative. Often, this includes generating performance measurements from *only* their current customers and not considering the value of debriefing former customers, competitors' customers, intermediate customers, and their own staff as part of the process.

Even in industries seemingly not impacted by loyalty, such as electric utilities, approaching deregulation will render satisfaction objectives less important than finding ways to keep their customers.

Superficial how-are-we-doing? questionnaires will not help companies keep customers. A national discount clothing chain uses in-store, mail-back comment cards (this is a highly ineffective way to generate objective customer data and it will be discussed later in the book) asking customers to give a report card grade on 16 different performance attributes, but doesn't ask about future purchase likelihood. One of the attributes is "having a good variety of merchandise." If customers rate the store at a medium to high level of satisfaction, and then defect because the store doesn't have their shirt or dress sizes in quantity, there is no way for the retailer to get this information. In fact, what has it really learned about its performance?

Customer measurement systems are not extremely difficult. If the measurement goal is satisfaction or the generation of an artificial index built around satisfaction, even the best designed system will give the company ineffective, even erroneous direction.

There is another potential mistake companies can make with measurement systems. These systems may not provide information that translates into operational process improvement. The system must facilitate operational deployment.

The Five Cures

If it is true, as Newton postulated, that every action has an equal and opposite reaction, and that even Ebenezer Scrooge, by changing his ways and finding redemption, can become better, it is within every company's ability to have more effective customer product and service performance measurement systems. The common element is proaction. Appropriate actionable questions must be asked.

1. Gather Latent and Registered Complaints

It isn't difficult to generate a full inventory of customer complaints within the measurement system. Just ask your customers. Companies can include a battery of questions addressing complaints.

- What are they? Can they be categorized?
- Have they been brought to the company's attention? To whom (sales representative, customer service, service management, and so on) and with what result (degree of closure)?
- Are there any complaints that haven't been communicated to the company? What are they? Why weren't they communicated?

This is a general framework for complaint questions. Company complaint measurement systems can be more specific, if needed.

The complaint questions can also be an opportunity to interact directly with complaining customers, obtain anecdotal information, and make tactical improvement. Complaint questions should, of course, also be asked of former customers, competitors' customers, intermediate customers, and staff. This contributes to both competitive strategy development and operational upgrade.

A furniture manufacturer may receive complaints about (1) order back-up or (2) slow delivery. Their measurement system may also reveal that there (3) are product quality or (4) packaging problems that haven't been expressed. Any of these four complaint areas could contribute to customer attrition. It's equally possible that none of them do. This will only be known once analysis has been completed.

2. Identify and Measure Critical Incidents and Transactions

The higher the level of service required or product and service requirements combined, the more important it becomes to measure the impact of specific customer-provider transactions.

When a customer goes to the supermarket, there may be dozens of specific critical incidents or transactions between the customer and the service provider and the products it stocks. Similarly, when a customer goes to the movies on Saturday night, there may also be scores of separate customer-provider transactions.

The typical measurement system attributes ("hospitality," "having good quality merchandise," "speed of checkout," or "cleanliness") offer a first level of detail, at best. If the supermarket is to make real improvement, how can this be done without knowing that its stock coverage is insufficient for customers who shop on weekends and that some of the products aren't always fresh? How can the movie theater improve its service if it doesn't understand how much customers resent having to wait in long lines for tickets, or how much they dislike hearing sounds from adjoining theaters?

Companies must first learn from customers what these critical incidents are; then they must incorporate them into the measurement system; and, finally, like complaints, they must take customers' assessment of critical incident performance and importance and correlate them to customers' level of loyalty.

3. Include Customer Expectations

Since many areas of performance are so closely related to specific customer expectation—time, accuracy, price, and durability or reliability—companies must first identify standards of acceptability for each expectation area. In the measurement system itself, these standards can be quantified to see if specific customer groups (by age, sex, purchase volume, or types of purchases) find them more acceptable or less acceptable. Then, like complaints, their assessments should be analyzed and correlated to potential future purchase activity.

4. Pay Attention to Customer-Provider Gaps

It would be the rare company, indeed, that has perfect alignment between customers' perceptions of product and service delivery and what is actually being delivered by staff. Still, the goal of staff-customer alignment is an essential building block of a customer-retention focus.

If staff is regularly included as part of the customer product and service performance measurement system, the company will be able to (1) identify where perceptual gaps exist between customers and staff and perceived delivery, (2) determine which, if any, of the gaps are contributing to attrition or defection, and (3) plan training and improvement programs accordingly.

Perceptual alignment should not be limited to customer-facing staff. The more management levels in any organization, the greater the need for managers who are distant from customers to create regular interaction opportunities with customers and the greater the benefit to include them in the measurement process. The study of gaps at multiple organizational levels, in addition to the objective of keeping customers, provides intermediate values such as improving vertical and horizontal information flow. For example, gap assessment can identify where management and staff disagree on quality of product and service delivery and where there is inconsistency on delivery policies between departments or groups. These can then be targeted for improvement.

5. Develop Models for Customer Retention

When a company focuses on customer satisfaction, in lieu of customer retention and loyalty, its delivery measurement systems generally reflect this concentration. Deficiencies can occur in any of several areas. First, does it include only current customers in measurement? Second, does it have a complete profile of customer needs and complaints? Third, is staff part of the measurement system? Fourth, does it examine specific areas of delivery transaction? Fifth, and most important, is it asking customers about future purchase/usage intent and likelihood to recommend the company's products or services?

  ✓ Loyalty and recommendation questions must be included. Without them, relationships cannot be developed between purchase intention and customer and staff perceptions, complaints, or delivery specifics. These relationships are used to create actionable priority models. The priority models, in turn, drive training, communication, marketing, sales, operational, and other activities.

  Finally, as mentioned earlier, models and other system-based analyses should be readily applied to improvement activities. Knowing should become doing.

Exercise

Twentieth Century's customer satisfaction measurement instrument has been a simple two-page annual mail survey conducted among only current customers. The questionnaire was designed over ten years ago and hasn't been modified since. The bank president has expressed the feeling that data from the system could be much more actionable. Little training or operational change comes as a result of the bank's study.

  What deficiencies, if any, do you see with the current measurement system, and what changes, if any, would you make? Address objectives, the measurement system itself, and operational applications of the data.

Summary

Many customer product and service performance measurement systems have one, or more, areas of deficiency. They

1. Follow rather than lead customers.

2. Consider only registered complaints and ignore latent ones.

3. Measure only global attributes, not operational elements or delivery transactions.

4. Ignore customer expectations.

5. Ignore customer-provider gaps.

6. Have a measurement goal of customer satisfaction.

In addition, measurement systems may not be adequately set up to facilitate data deployment throughout the organization.

Notes

1. John A. Goodman, Scott M. Broetzmann, and Colin Adamson, "Ineffective—That's the Problem with Customer Satisfaction Surveys," *Quality Progress* (May 1992): 35–38.

2. *Ideals of the Samurai,* William Scott Wilson trans. (Burbank, Calif.: Ohara Publications, 1982), 92.

3. Frederick F. Reichheld, "Loyalty-Based Management," *Harvard Business Review,* (March–April 1993): 67.

4. Denis Walker, *Customer First* (Brookfield, Vt.: Gower, 1990), 9.

5. Valarie A. Zeithaml, A. Parasuraman and Leonard L. Berry, *Delivering Quality Service* (New York: The Free Press, 1990), 19.

6. Walker, *Customer First,* 9.

Chapter 4

Evaluating Latent
and Registered Complaints

*Of all dissatisfied customers, only around 5 percent actually make a
complaint. Of those complaints, many can be answered satisfactorily
by a clarification of the situation. Most of the rest can be answered
through negotiation. Only a few of the customers who complain cannot be re-established as supporters of your product or service. All the
rest offer an opportunity to correct and learn. Doing it well can actually enhance your service reputation. Future business depends on
reputation.*[1]

—Denis Walker, *Customer First*

The Strategic Limitations of Registered
Complaint Systems

Some companies have taken extraordinary measures to give customers
the opportunity of voicing questions, problems, and complaints. They
have installed 24-hour, 800-number complaint hotlines, extended customer service hours, and let customers know who they can contact
through special mailings, product handbooks, and instruction sheets.
Examples include

- CSX Transportation, through its customer service center in
  Florida, monitors called-in problems and complaint trends
  through a service quality report. It uses the report to address
  how the complaints were handled and why they occurred.

- Dun & Bradstreet has set up Duns Net, a worldwide
  telecommunication network, to support its on-line information
  product.

- General Electric Company's GE Answer Center, open 365 days
  a year, receives complaints and questions about GE products. It
  gets thousands of calls a week.

- Honeywell has a Customer Response Center. Within the center
  is the Technical Assistance Center, which is staffed 24 hours a

day, seven days a week. It receives several hundred calls each week.

- Polaroid has the Polaroid Resource Center and 800-line problem and complaint service in five regional offices around the United States.

- Burger King's 24-hour call-in service receives input from several thousand customers per day. When a percentage of the calls reaches a certain level, the system prompts investigation and resolution. One-quarter of complaining customers are called back within a month to close the loop or reinforce satisfaction with their call.

- Eastman Chemical Company has a complaints handling process, which begins with a database of all received complaints. Complaints are then assigned to a customer advocate, and the resolution of each complaint is monitored.

- Sears has an 800-number to handle customer inquiries on a local basis as a means of ensuring customer satisfaction. Once a contact has been received, the inquiry is supposed to be resolved within 30 minutes. All customer inquiries and resolutions are monitored by Sears' National Customer Relations Office.

- United Van Lines follows up on negative customer moving experiences (communicated by mail) through a management team.

- GM and Ford, along with many other vehicle manufacturers, have a special customer advocate telephone number to call for car performance difficulties or dealer disputes.

- The major auto rental companies, while asking customers about their vehicle's performance, rarely capture the feedback or take action when negatives are expressed.

Each of these companies has built systems and created infrastructure to support these complaint-handling efforts. Some have gone further. They have used these systems to generate statistical models of complaint, which then translate into improvement priorities and programs.

Even the best of these systems must be considered of somewhat limited value, however. While the customer is given the opportunity to express complaints in many delivery situations, the reality is that few customers will ever voluntarily register a complaint.

Customers who complain are usually motivated by anger, frustration, or the like with a product and/or service, and its performance has to be low enough, or inconvenience them enough, to have them make the supplier aware of their concerns. The vast majority of customers will not take the time, do not want the confrontation, or feel the company will do nothing about their complaint anyway. So they don't complain. Frequently, they just leave without ever telling the supplier why they left. In leaving, they tell 10 to 20 friends, colleagues, or relatives about their complaints. Also, their unexpressed complaints are often different than those communicated to the company through other methods.

When only registered complaints are used, it's a bit like using an incompletely drawn map for directions. The intention is there, but the accuracy isn't. A company working from registered complaints only has part of the story and is missing the most important parts of the map.

Customers who complain may have profoundly different purchase, demographic, and even personality traits from those who don't. Registered complaints may be largely unrepresentative of problems and difficulties customers are experiencing. Registered complaints are inadequate for identifying the depth or the extent of customer problems. The bottom line on registered complaints is that no matter how good the monitoring system, they inadequately and incompletely support a corporate goal of optimal customer retention. As Henry Kissinger advised his party at the 1980 Republican convention, "If we don't know where we're going, any road we take will get us there." The only actionable complaint road map is one that includes all complaints, both registered and unregistered.

Proactively Eliciting Complaints

When companies have a complete profile, or inventory, of *all* customer complaints, that is, complaints generated through the reactive channels just described and complaints generated nonvoluntarily, then they can act on complaints with greater certainty. What they often fail to recognize, and this can be a fatal failure, is that most complaints are below the surface and are unknown. This is the Iceberg Complaint Model (see Figure 4.1).

Customers have a wide variety of reasons for their complaints. They may have had poor experience with product quality or service. They may have had negatives with an element of service such as sales representative accessibility, customer service knowledge and responsiveness, delivery scheduling or timing, order completeness, or billing accuracy and the like. They may even have had negative experience with a previously expressed complaint.

What is certain, and has been demonstrated in study after study, is that, even if strongly motivated, most customers do not complain. It

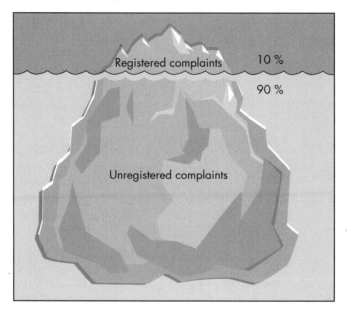

Source: ARBOR, Inc., 1994.

Figure 4.1. Iceberg Complaint Model.

can also be said with some certainty that the less loyal customers are to a supplier—in other words the more they are in an attrition mode and in the process of defecting—the less likely they are to complain. Also, the less direct involvement or transaction with a supplier, the less likely they are to complain. Their imagined investment in the supplier company has decreased to a level that doesn't support making the effort to complain.

Some complaints contribute directly to attrition and defection, others less or not at all. The complaints of customers in an attrition mode are often more serious and compelling than those of good, solid, loyal customers. Similarly, the complaints of customers who have already left are often a reflection of why less loyal customers are heading for the door.

How does a company go about generating latent complaints? There are two principal opportunities: customer contact situations and the customer measurement system.

Customer Contact

Customer contact is any sales or service situation in which the customer is in a position to provide information. This can occur in a sales call, a customer visit, customer round tables and forums, or product/service delivery situations. Unexpressed complaints can even be generated within a complaint call simply by asking for additional depth on the expressed complaint or for other, unexpressed complaints.

Most businesses are not set up to generate latent complaints when contact situations arise. Sales, front-line service staff, and even management have little or no training in how to ask for and capture such knowledge, so the opportunities are squandered, and the company misses a valuable source of information.

An example that many active business people can relate to is that of rental car returns. Rental car staff are trained to ask the customer how the vehicle performed when the car is returned. For years, when asked, we have been saying that "the driver's side mirror has a lot of water spots, which makes it difficult to use." This has generated little more than an occasional "I'm sorry to hear that" to my colleagues and I. None of the counter staff has ever written down the complaint, said they would do anything about it, or proactively offered to give any of us some incentive to use their service again (such as a reduced rate or free rental). Though purportedly empowered to act on behalf of the customer, they have not done so.

Customer complaints generated through routine or special contact should be organized and acted upon. Before latent complaint data can be used, however, they must first be captured. This may require readdressing the company's culture, staff training priorities, or both.

Customer Measurement Systems

However the company generates perceptual and evaluative information from customers, product or service complaint questioning should be a part of the process. It has its own question section within a questionnaire.

The company needs to identify what complaints customers have registered with the company and how those complaints have been resolved. Of equal or greater importance, however, is identifying the complaints that have thus far gone unregistered, the reasons customers have not raised them, and the person or department to whom this heretofore unregistered complaint should now be directed.

Evaluating the Loyalty Impact of Complaints

As mentioned earlier, complaints can have high, moderate, or low impact on customer loyalty. While companies will want to proactively act on all complaints, as a practical matter they should receive attention on a priority basis. Within the analysis, companies can look at the inventory of complaints to articulate and determine how they correlate with each other and how they correlate with the objective of keeping the customer.

In chapter 2, the relationship between customer loyalty and expressed/resolved, expressed/unresolved, and unexpressed complaints was discussed using a retail hardware chain's current and former customer research results as a demonstration of loyalty impact. Focusing on floor service time as an issue, current customers were more positively disposed to the chain when their complaint had been registered and resolved. The greater percentages of these customers had not expressed the complaint in the store or to customer service personnel, however, and the effect on customer attrition and loss was much stronger.

Another way to look at complaints is how well staff, frontline or management, understands both the level and the effect of complaints. This is an alignment issue.

Using the same example from chapter 2, store managers were asked what percent of customers have complaints about time to get floor service. They said 5 percent. This compares to 22 percent of current customers (9 percent who had expressed this as a complaint, 13 percent who had the complaint but hadn't expressed it) and fully 43 percent of former customers (14 percent registered, 29 percent unregistered).[2] This disparity is shown in Figure 4.2.

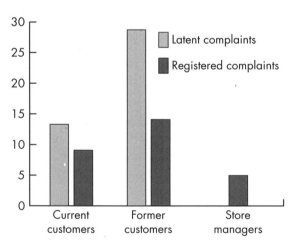

Source: ARBOR, Inc., 1991.

Figure 4.2. Latent/registered complaints profile.

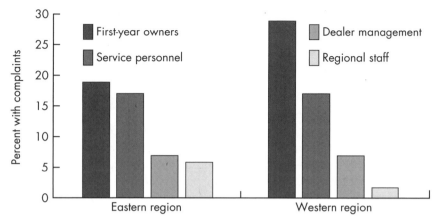

Source: ARBOR, Inc., 1991.

Figure 4.3. Service or repairs complaints gap profile.

Chapter 6 presents the perceived differences in service delivery between new car owners, dealership sales and management, and regional company staff. Figure 4.3 shows differences between perceived complaint levels by first-year car owners (by dealership service and management staff, and regional company staff) in two regions and the actual first-year owner complaints in those regions.

The figure represents only the expressed, or registered, complaints by first-year owners. As in many other examples, latent, or unregistered, service and repair complaints were from a much higher percentage of customers. Of greater concern was that these unregistered complaints translated directly into probable customer loss for the dealerships and the manufacturer involved.

While it is valuable to identify the perceptual differences, or gaps, between company staff and customers on complaint issues, it is vital that the loyalty impact of complaints be understood so that they can be prioritized for improvement activity.

Acting on Complaints

Companies viewing complaints as opportunities for improved customer relationships and improved products and services will (1) want to take some sort of action on the complaints, and (2) want to have an efficient and nonbureaucratic structure for receiving, collecting, communicating, and following-up on complaints.

Complaints have both tactical and strategic implications for a company. In the short term, they need to be addressed and acted upon so that customers' expectations of the supplier remains high and so that the customer is made to feel that the supplier appreciates concerns and problems being made evident.

The company can respond to complaints either passively or proactively. Passive response is very much in the satisfaction mode, in which the inclination is to quickly mollify the customer or get feedback, but not take any really corrective action.

Proactive response, on the other hand, puts the company in a customer partnership, customer-retention mode encouraging communication and interaction. Problems will be fixed at minimum, but the company uses complaints—expressed voluntarily or not—to respond in a customer-planning manner. In the auto rental example presented earlier in the chapter, frontline employees could respond to a complaint by taking full notes on the cause and be empowered to offer the customer delightful, even exciting service, as a reward for bringing the complaint to their attention.

Tactical complaint proaction also means that customer-facing employees are selected based on sensitivity to people and that they are trained to get at the roots of customer concerns. They should express empathy and seek to find solutions acceptable, or better, to the customer. Again, tactical complaint responses are opportunities to either reinforce or diminish loyalty.

On a strategic level, complaints should be systematized into an action process, with the company prioritizing action based on the potential and actual effect of the complaint on customer loyalty. A simple structure can be created, by which one department acts as the receiving, assessment, recommendation, and action center for all complaints. It would maintain and coordinate a complaints database, detailed as to type, location, and severity of the complaint. Rather than handle all complaints in an ad hoc, firefighting manner, the company can respond tactically, as needed, but within a strategic framework.

Companies with reputations for excellent service such as L. L. Bean and Nordstrom have this reputation and consequently keep good customers longer, in part, because they have preventive tactical and strategic processes in place to plan for, identify, and take action on virtually any complaints. Frontline staff at these companies have the authority (and training) to resolve all but the most difficult problems with products or service.

Exercise

Twentieth Century National trains service representatives and branch managers to solicit complaints from customers. There is no indication as to how this is working because Twentieth Century does not include complaint questions in its customer measurement system. Further, branch service and management staff are given little latitude as to complaint response. So, they don't know if, or how, complaints are impacting customer retention.

Begin planning for both a strategic and tactical approach to customer complaints, at both corporate and branch levels.

Summary

Companies have built complaint systems around expressed, or registered, complaints. Registered complaints represent only the tip of the iceberg of all customers' complaints. Without identifying unexpressed, or latent, complaints, companies may make improvement errors or otherwise inefficiently apply resources.

Latent complaints can be generated through all customer contact, or transaction, points, plus the company's ongoing customer measurement program.

Complaints requiring the most attention are those having the greatest potential impact on customer loyalty. This requires both a full inventory and database of complaints plus thorough analysis of relationships between attrition and expressed/unexpressed complaints.

Action on complaints is done tactically, with well-trained, customer-sensitive staff, and strategically, with systems in place to help set and direct improvement priorities.

Notes

1. Denis Walker, *Customer First* (Brookfield, Vt.: Gower, 1990), 12–13.

2. Based on ARBOR customer service research study.

Chapter 5

Identifying Customer Needs, Expectations, and Problems and Gauging Their Impact

It is not good to settle into a set of opinions. It is a mistake to put forth effort and obtain some understanding and then stop at that. . . . Do not rely on following the degree of understanding that you have discovered, but simply think, "This is not enough."[1]

—Hagakure, *The Book of the Samurai*

Marketing is the performance of those activities which seek to accomplish an organizational objective by anticipating customer or client needs and directing a flow of need satisfying goods and services from producer to customer or client.[2]

—Professor E. Jerome McCarthy, Michigan State University

Companies don't sell products, but rather the expertise and the technologies to help users define their needs and create the products best suited for them.[3]

—Ken Gerlach, Hewlett-Packard Company

What Are Customer Needs, Expectations, and Problems, and Why Are They the Most Critical Elements of a Customer Retention Focus?

Needs, expectations, and problems are the basic and common denominators of customer retention.

Needs

As stated by C. Glenn Walters and Gordon W. Paul, "The foundations for consumer behavior rest on needs, for without needs, consumers would never have a reason to purchase."[4] Abbie Griffin and

45

John Hauser identified needs as "in a description, in the customer's own words, of the benefits to be fulfilled by the product or service."[5] When they have been identified and their specific effect on customer retention determined, prescriptive action can be taken. It must also be remembered, however, that they are constantly changing. Companies must understand both current and emerging customer needs to remain competitive.

In the personal computer industry, for example, customers' desires for more powerful and versatile software is driving hardware manufacturers to develop computers with more speed and capacity, at an attractive price. In the automotive industry, recent years have seen crush zones, anti-lock braking systems, and four-wheel drive as a response to safety needs and freon-free air-conditioning to reduce the impact of autos on the ozone layer.

For product and service providers alike, one of the biggest and ongoing concerns is: What will customers want next? The importance of this knowledge cannot be overstressed. As stated by Zeithaml, Parasuraman, and Berry in *Delivering Quality Service*[6]

> Being a little bit wrong about what customers want can mean losing a customer's business when another company hits the target exactly. Being a little bit wrong can mean expending money, time and other resources on things that don't count to customers. Being a little bit wrong can even mean not surviving in a fiercely competitive market.

Expectations

Dr. Richard C. H. Chua of Anderson Consulting has identified a customer-driven definition of quality as, "Quality is continuously anticipating and exceeding the requirements and expectations of customers."[7] Following this definition, product and service companies have to develop an understanding of what customers expect. Expectations are frequently dimensional in nature: time, size, price, frequency, weight, completeness, and so on.

Problems

Problems are those customer opinions, attitudes, and beliefs that result from the company's inability to appropriately address, meet, or exceed their needs and expectations. These are product or service performance areas that, while important to customers, are not being delivered well by providers. They are frequently emerging areas of complaint and may be only partially formed in the customer's mind; however, they actively contribute to attrition and defection. Like needs and expectations, they must be identified and included in an action process.

Need Identification and Assessment

Understanding customer needs is certainly not a new phenomenon. In the West, it can be traced back to English philosopher, jurist, and economist Jeremy Bentham. In his 1789 *Table of Springs of Action Showing the Various Species of Pleasures and Pains of Which Man's Nature Is Susceptible*, he listed money, power, safety, and curiosity among human needs.[8] Some 150 years before that the first member of the Mitsui family, a merchant in Edo (now Tokyo), Japan, opened a store with household and other goods based on his identification of his customers' wants and desires.

Freud, among others, also looked at individual needs in his studies. (Note: To avoid confusing readers with similar ideas like *wants, desires, drives, wishes,* and *motives* with needs, and since there appears to be far less than total agreement among psychologists and sociologists as to their individual definitions, *needs* will be the common term used throughout). In the 1930s and 1940s, as advertising and marketing became increasingly more prominent as disciplines, customer needs were still expressed in largely psychological, rather than sociological, terms.

It was not until 1954, however, that the most representative list of needs was identified. Dr. Abraham H. Maslow, in *Motivation and Personality,* identified a seven-element need hierarchy that is still used today by marketers and researchers (see Figure 5.1).

Practically (rather than psychologically) speaking, needs and their classification or identification can be thought of in three ways: time, state, and level.

1. *Time*
   –*Existing* needs—The current lack of something that is wanted. Existing needs are generally of a conscience nature, such as reliability or safety.
   –*Future* needs—These needs do not currently exist, but may be emerging or presenting themselves because of technological or societal changes. Energy-saving devices and faster, cheaper computers with more features are two examples.

2. *State*
   –*Emotional* needs—Nonrational and subjective in nature, these needs may have to do with self-image, status, and aesthetics. The changing palette of automobile colors over the years is an example of manufacturers meeting emotional needs.
   –*Rational* needs—These are functional and utilitarian in nature. Cordless vacuums, drills, and other tools have gained strong

Figure 5.1. Maslow's hierarchy of needs.

market response in recent years, as have telephone services
(call waiting and so on), reflecting consumers' desire for convenience.

3. *Level*
   –*Primary* needs—These are the more basic needs in Maslow's
   hierarchy, such as physical and psychological. They are important enough that the customer must meet or exceed them to
   maintain a normal existence. These include food, shelter, relationships, and exercise.
   –*Secondary* needs—Those needs that might be useful or helpful
   to the customer, but are not essential. Attractiveness, convenience, and comfort are included among secondary needs.

   Griffin and Hauser identify needs as *basic* (what a customer assumes the product or service will do), *articulated* (what a customer
wants the product or service to do), and *exciting* (what a customer
would find delightful or surprising if done by the product or service).[9]
This progression is not dissimilar from that of the Kano model.

It is fair to say that these methods of viewing needs can never be done in isolation. Needs are complex in nature, constantly in conflict, and continuously evolving. As Professor John Quelch of Harvard has said, "Services that are top priority at the time of sale may be less important five years later. Companies must understand the pattern and timing of demand for customer services."[10] This complexity makes it imperative that customers be segmented. What is a primary and rational need to one customer, such as the way to choose an automobile, bank, dry cleaner, or business products supplier, may easily be a secondary and emotional need to another customer. Future needs today may be existing needs tomorrow.

Customers assign priorities to their needs, frequently because, in making a purchase or choosing a service, the customer will not see all needs fulfilled equally, and so will make compromises and trade-offs. In these decisions, some needs are fully realized, some partial, and some not at all. Every decision is, to some extent, a reflection of an abridgement of Maslow's hierarchy.

When needs cannot be fulfilled by a product or service or are only minimally fulfilled, customers may repress them in several ways. In other words, they may rationalize that those needs are unnecessary. More frequently, however, these unmet needs result in customer frustration, and the frustration frequently leads directly to attrition or defection. If needs are constantly changing and evolving, it is also true that they are neverending. Product or service suppliers failing to recognize this have or will put their businesses in jeopardy. Need determination can be considered as a simplified five-point model or process. In order of processing, these are

- Identification—How customers perceive needs or requirements.
- Clarification—Distillation into common and customer-defined elements.
- Evaluation—Needs are condensed into product or service characteristics.
- Specification—Importance and priority are determined.
- Updating—Needs are readdressed at intervals to keep pace with industrial and societal change.

Companies can identify customer needs by making use of existing information such as sales reports or customer service feedback. They can also come from outside sources, such as public or government studies and industry experts. The most complete and actionable information, though more difficult and expensive to obtain, comes from the customers themselves.

Companies should go through a needs audit or inventory to determine the full range of customer needs. Because most businesses are not brand-new, before beginning such an inventory, the company should look at

- Their own product and service objectives
- What products and services they already provide
- What the competition provides
- What product and service trade-offs they believe their customers will make
- What level of importance they (believe they) can already ascribe to certain customer needs

The needs inventory can be developed through a systematized approach to qualitative research. Identification of needs and their importance comes from interviewing customers one-on-one for 30 to 60 minutes; through minigroups (five to six customers for an hour); from full focus groups (8–12 customers for two hours); or some combination of these approaches. A broad range of projective techniques—life cycle experience, laddering, and so on—can be applied to elicit needs.

Design of qualitative studies should be sufficient to identify needs from all major customer segments. Typically, 10 focus groups or 20 to 30 one-on-one interviews will be sufficient to generate a full customer-needs inventory (usually, 200 to 400+ needs are identified). Figure 5.2, based on work by Silver and Thompson, shows the percentage of needs identified by each technique.

Note that, although the company has created a database of customer needs at this point, this is qualitative information and does not indicate concentration or priority by customer group. Before needs information can be applied to quality improvement efforts, quantification of needs must first be accomplished.

Evaluating Expectations

Expectations are closely related to needs, except they can usually be stated in more finite terms, such as the number of hours for completion of an equipment repair or the size of a main course portion at a restaurant. They are, then, more fully formed, like a product or service attribute.

Expectation level typically has been identified by attaching an importance score or value to the product or service performance characteristic;

ex: guantifying saturation

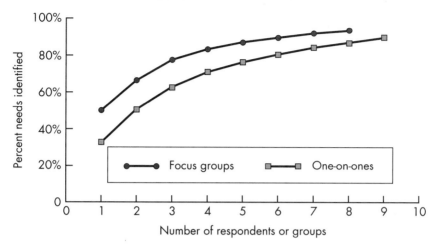

Source: Silver, Jonathan Alan and Thompson, John Charles, Jr. ,"Understanding Customer Needs: A Systematic Approach to the 'Voice of the customer'" (Cambridge, Ma: M.S. Thesis, Massachusetts Institute of Technology, Sloan School of Management, 1991) per Abbie Griffin and John R. Hauser. "The Voice of the Customer," *Marketing Science* 12 (Winter 1993): 8.

Figure 5.2. Focus groups vs. one-on-one interviews for office equipment.

however, one of the recent and more useful techniques for understanding expectations is the Van Westendorp methodology. This unique procedure was originally developed by Dutch economist Peter H. Van Westendorp to identify optimal prices for products and services.[11] We have adapted it for understanding customer preferences and tolerances of service issues (response times, order and billing efficiency, and so on) and product elements (failure/defect rates).

Using service response time as an illustrative example, data for the Van Westendorp technique come from a simple series of four questions.

• How long a response time would you find to be appropriate or acceptable?

• How long a service response time would make you feel bothered or inconvenienced?

• How long a service response time would be too slow, so lengthy that you would likely contact some other (product or service) provider?

• How long a service response time would you find too fast, so fast that you would question the reliability of the service?

These questions would be carefully pretested in focus groups or other qualitative research in which other demanded customer needs are developed and over the telephone in preliminary phases of customer service (or product) research questionnaire development. Quantitative research instruments and methods will be discussed later in the book.

Respondents typically work with a scale of 10 to 30 response times (or performance rates) spaced equally apart. For example, we might use a scale that starts at one hour and goes by half hours up to 12 hours. (This could also be easily executed over the phone by asking customers to look at a clock or watch for reference.) These data are evaluated by plotting the cumulative frequency distribution for each question on a graph where short to long response times are located along the horizontal axis and (cumulative) percent of respondents is located on the vertical axis. (See Figure 5.3.)

Customer Expectation for Response Time

The customer expectation for an acceptable response time is found by plotting responses to the "acceptable" and the "bothered" questions. In this service example, almost everyone would be comfortable with a two-hour response time and only a few would be comfortable with a 10-hour wait. Conversely, only 10 percent would actually be bothered by a three-hour response time, and, at nine hours, almost everyone would be bothered.

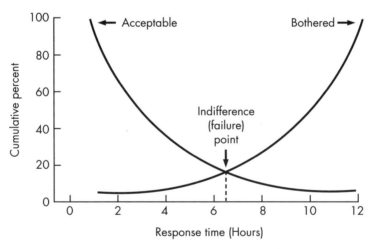

Source: Adapted by John Wittenbroker, ARBOR, Inc., from Daniel C. Lockhart and Roger Tourangeau, "The Effect of Suggested Price Points on Open-Ended Price Estimates," Presentation: *Society for Consumer Psychology APA Annual Convention*, 1992, pp. 59–65, and Kenneth M. Travis, "Price Sensitivity Measurement Technique Plots Product Price vs. Quality Perceptions," *Marketing News*, 14 May 1982, p. 4.

Figure 5.3. Van Westendorp analysis expectation for response time.

The customer expectation for response time is found at the intersection of these two curves. The point of the intersection, at six-and-a-half hours in the example, is termed the indifference point, or failure point, and is the response time at which the percent of respondents who are comfortable (25 percent) is equal to the percent who are bothered (25 percent). The remaining 50 percent of respondents are indifferent to this response time; the six-and-one-half hour response time fell between their "acceptable" response and their "bothered" response.

We identify the indifference point as the customer expectation because it is the point at which the trade-off between accommodating customers and bothering or inconveniencing them occurs. This would roughly correspond to "one-dimensional quality" identified in the Kano model; however, it frequently identifies a service delivery minimum, or standard, below which companies may find it difficult to recoup customer confidence or loyalty.

Range of Acceptable Response Times

A range of "acceptable" response times can also be identified by plotting the cumulative distributions from the "too slow" and "too fast" questions along with the reverses (1%) of the "satisfactory" and "bother" curves. (See Figure 5.4.)

In summary, the location of the indifference point on the horizontal scale represents the customer-based standard or expectation for service response time. If response times are longer, more people will be bothered than accommodated. If response time are faster, more people will be accommodated than bothered, but this can come at an increased expense of staff, time and equipment cost.

Companies can use this type of analysis to segment customers by expectation level and identify the degree to which they will accommodate them by expending resources.

Locating Problems

Problems can occur any time an area of product or service performance or service transaction is important to customers but is being poorly achieved by the provider. The customer may not experience it as a problem or may not be able to articulate it as a problem; however, it represents performance softness or vulnerability and can lead to attrition or defection.

With a regular schedule or mechanism of objective customer feedback (qualitative and quantitative interviewing) plus the company's own system of customer information (salesperson reports, customer

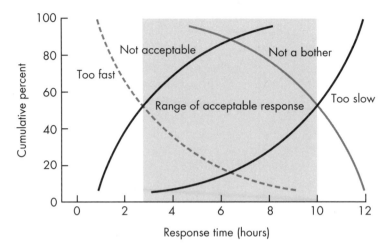

Source: Adapted by John Wittenbroker, ARBOR, Inc., from Daniel C. Lockhart and Roger Tourangeau, "The Effect of Suggested Price Points on Open-Ended Price Estimates," Presentation: *Society for Consumer Psychology APA Annual Convention*, 1992. pp. 59–65 and Kenneth M. Travis, "Price Sensitivity Measurement Technique Plots Product Price vs. Quality Perceptions," *Marketing News*, May 14, 1982, p. 4.

Figure 5.4. Van Westendorp analysis range of acceptable response times.

service reports, service lines), problem areas can be identified early enough to prevent them from becoming complaints. A quadrant analysis (a very useful device for identifying areas of potential performance problems) shows how customers view product or service attribute performance and importance and is called a Customer Action Window[SM].

Customer Action Window[SM] will identify which attributes, relative to all other areas of delivery, are highly important but are not being performed well. This would be shown in the upper left quadrant of the Customer Action Window[SM] in Figure 5.5.

The other potential problem area for a company is in the lower right quadrant "customer does not want it and gets it anyway." This is a performance attribute to which the company has devoted some resources. Customers rate these attributes as high on performance but don't ascribe equally high importance. Thus, that attribute is either *really* not important or the company has not appropriately communicated its value to customers. If a merchant offers customers free coffee and doughnuts in the morning, but (1) customers don't ascribe any value to this service or (2) the merchant hasn't used an advertising slogan like "We start your day right!" to promote this service to customers, the expense should likely be reviewed to see if better uses can be made for the money.

Source: ARBOR, Inc., 1991.

Figure 5.5. Customer Action Window[SM].

By way of illustration, we present the following hypothetical example of an industrial products company which received high importance and low performance scores for "product quality/defect rate" and also for "customer service/responsiveness" and "product modification flexibility (see Figure 5.6). Of the 12 performance attributes measured, these three were the potential problem areas.

Other areas, such as "product development leadership," were not considered important by customers, even though the company had an active R&D program.

Exercise

In interviewing current and former customers, Twentieth Century National identifies a need built around customer convenience and access. Upstart State Bank is a small, relatively new competitor with several branches in one of the regions where Twentieth Century has experienced the greatest customer loss. It is the only bank offering Saturday hours (10 A.M. to 6 P.M.), with full teller and drive-through service during those hours. Customers' need for convenience has been elevated to an expectation by Upstart, and Twentieth Century's current customers now perceive their Monday–Friday, 9 A.M.–3 P.M. hours as important and not performed well by Twentieth Century, hence an emerging problem.

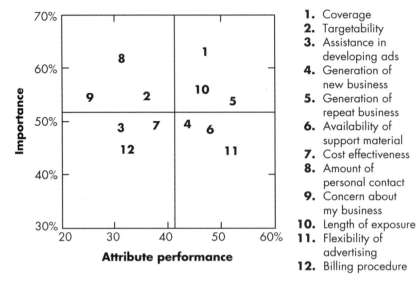

1. Coverage
2. Targetability
3. Assistance in developing ads
4. Generation of new business
5. Generation of repeat business
6. Availability of support material
7. Cost effectiveness
8. Amount of personal contact
9. Concern about my business
10. Length of exposure
11. Flexibility of advertising
12. Billing procedure

Source: ARBOR, Inc., 1994.

Figure 5.6. Print media company Customer Action Window[SM].

How can Twentieth Century address this issue and gain back the advantage?

Summary

Identifying and understanding customer needs, expectations, and problems is essential to a customer-retention focus. Needs can be classified according to a hierarchy and according to time (existing or future), state (emotional or rational), or level (primary or secondary). Customers, as part of the supplier decision process, prioritize and make trade-offs between their sets of needs. Companies can develop an inventory of their customers' needs.

Expectations are more finite requirements and tolerances for a performance area. Acceptable and unacceptable performance can be modeled to create an expectation level. Problems can emerge when an important performance area is seen as not being performed well.

Notes

1. Yamamoto Tsunetomo, Hagakure: *The Book of the Samurai* (Tokyo: Kodansha International, 1979), 31.

2. Al Ries and Jack Trout, *Marketing Warfare* (New York: McGraw-Hill, 1986), 2.

3. Ken Gerlach, "Is Marketing Research Enough?" *Sales and Marketing Strategies & News* (March 1991): 7+.

4. C. Glenn Walters and Gordon W. Paul, *Consumer Behavior* (Homewood, Ill.: Richard D. Irwin, 1970), 241.

5. Abbie Griffin and John R. Hauser, "The Voice of the Customer," *Marketing Science* 12, (Winter 1993): 4–5.

6. Valarie A. Zeithaml, A. Parasuraman, and Leonard L. Berry, *Delivering Quality Service* (New York: The Free Press, 1990), 51.

7. Richard C. H. Chua, "A Customer-Driven Approach for Measuring Service Quality," *1992 ASQC Quality Congress Transactions* (Milwaukee, Wis.: ASQC), 1196.

8. Sir Alexander Gray, *The Development of Economic Doctrine* (New York: John Wiley & Sons, 1961), 337; and Fred T. Schreier, *Modern Marketing Research* (Belmont, Calif.: Wadsworth Publishing Co., 1963), 281.

9. Griffin and Hauser, "The Voice of the Customer," 4–5.

10. John A. Quelch, *How to Market to Consumers* (New York: John Wiley & Sons, 1982), 29.

11. Adapted by ARBOR, Inc., from Daniel C. Lockhart and Roger Tourangeau, "The Effect of Suggested Price Points on Open-Ended Price Estimates" paper presented at Society for Consumer Psychology APA Annual Convention, Washington, D.C., August 1992, 59–64; and Kenneth M. Travis, "Price Sensitivity Measurement Technique Plots Product Price vs. Quality Perceptions," *Marketing News* (14 May 1982): 4.

Chapter 6

Customer-Provider Gaps

Consider the needs of your (customers) well, for it will be difficult to be wide of the mark when judging things in comparison from their standpoint.[1]
—Abridged Interpretation, Wall Inscription, Lord Nabeshima, Daimyo of Hizen, (1538–1618)

Managers may not know about certain service features critical to meeting customers' desires; or, even when aware of such features, they may not know which levels of performance customers desire along those features.[2]
—Zeithaml, Parasuraman, and Berry, *Delivering Quality Service*

The Importance of Gaps and Alignment

How well do those who *serve* the customer understand and align with the customer's needs, expectations, problems, and complaints? And why is the goal of alignment so critically important a part of customer retention?

Consider this example that many adults with school-age children get to experience. Little Jimmy (the end customer) is a fifth-grade student at Limitless Horizons Public Elementary School. He is an A student and has always been happy with his teachers. After two months, he regularly complains to you, his parent (the intermediate customer), that his teacher, Ms. Demeanor (the internal customer/service provider) is doing a terrible job teaching him history, English, and math. He says he isn't learning anything and he is unhappy. You enter a state of attrition and begin thinking about a form of defection, changing schools if the situation doesn't improve.

At Parent-Teacher night, Ms. Demeanor gives you an interpretation of lesson and curriculum delivery that is very different from Jimmy's. She says he is learning well and that he is a bright, happy student. Should you take your concerns to the principal or school board (internal

59

customer/management), you'll be even more confused. Whose interpretation is correct or accurate?

If you are a customer-driven parent, you would have to put Jimmy's education first. Assuming the situation didn't improve after further investigation and discussions with Jimmy and Ms. Demeanor, you might be forced to arrange for Jimmy to go to another school (defection).

Unlike products, services are not tangible, and they more frequently involve interaction between customers and providers. Also, although service may be continuous, customers often evaluate their level of service based on the last one or two contact occasions. Do those providing the service see what the customer sees, interpret the way the customer interprets? The perceptual differences between service providers, whether frontline or management, and customers is called a *gap*. Examining these important perceptual differences and narrowing or eliminating them is critical to customer retention.

What was true for Jimmy is equally true for any customer-provider relationship. Aligned customers and providers frequently (but not always) reflect an atmosphere of customer sensitivity and needs awareness. Nonaligned customers and providers, depending on the degree of perceptual gap between them, often indicate an atmosphere in which customer loyalty is a challenge.

If service providers separate themselves from customers, don't solicit customers' feedback, or fail to provide adequate mechanisms for customer input, the likelihood for customer-provider perceptual gap is high. Customer research studies have often shown a direct correlation between the lack of customer-provider alignment and customer attrition and defection. This appears true whether the provider is selling a product or service or whether that product or service competes in a consumer or business-to-business marketplace.

The difference between companies that are aligned with customers and those that are not is, again, *proaction,* the ability to identify customers' needs, expectations, complaints, and problems at an early point. At the very beginning of *In Search of Excellence*, Peters and Waterman identify eight basic principles for staying ahead of the competition.[3] Several deal specifically with customer proaction, responsiveness, and alignment.

- A bias for action. A preference for doing something, anything, rather than sending a question through cycles and cycles of analyses and committee reports.

- Staying close to the customer. Learning their preferences and catering to them.

- Autonomy and entrepreneurship. Breaking the corporation into small companies and encouraging staff to think independently and competitively.
- Hands-on, value-driven endeavors. Insisting that executives keep in touch with the firm's essential business.

Two companies recognizing the rewards of closing customer-provider gaps are Smith & Hawken and MBNA Corporation. Smith & Hawken's senior customer operations officer says, "One way you do this is to put yourself in the customer's place and see yourself as the customer. It absolutely works because it fulfills the customer need to hear what is going on." MBNA Corporation has all officers on regular monthly schedules monitoring customer service calls and combines this with an active research program to understand customer issues.

The common element in these examples is proaction. When companies realize that greater sales and profits come from retaining customers and that retaining them takes proactive customer focus and alignment—at all levels of the organization and in every act and decision—this becomes the basis for such change. In one research assignment evaluating a company's service culture, one division began every meeting—as mandated by the division general manager—by reviewing how that meeting will have an impact on the goal of keeping customers.

Having staff-customer perceptual gaps is potentially dangerous in any area of product or service delivery. If that delivery area affects, directly or indirectly, customer loyalty, the gaps may require immediate attention to hold down customer attrition or defection.

Earlier we discussed the impact of unexpressed complaints on loyalty. If a company is not proactively seeking to identify and correct customer concerns and complaints, it is missing an opportunity for alignment. Similarly, if customers are given few or no methods to interact with providers, or if customers *do* give input, such as through surveys, and the information is not deployed appropriately through the organization, the likelihood of customer-provider perceptual gaps will be increased.

An Alternative View of Perceptual Gaps

We in Western countries only recently have begun to understand the importance of customer-provider perceptual gaps. Japan has been studying gaps, or *suki,* and their meaning for hundreds of years. It has become an integral element in establishing and maintaining customer alignment.

In samurai times, the masters of strategy were called *gunpaisha*, keepers of large fans with information about their army, the opponent's army, and the terrain. The modern equivalent of gunpaisha are marketing, advertising, and sales planners, and frontline service staff who have current, in-depth, intimate knowledge of their products and services, competitors' products and services, the state of the marketplace, and customer needs and wants. With this detailed knowledge, they have the flexibility to apply many strategies and tactics, including

- *Ken no sen*—A bold strategy that propels a company into the lead. It assumes that competitors will not be able to meet the initiative.
  - In the late '60s and early '70s, the Franklin Mint literally created the mass market for limited edition collectibles. It had no real competition.
  - Eastman Kodak recently introduced an advanced compact zoom camera with portrait and panoramic features unavailable from any other manufacturer for the price. It did this through extensive customer research and involving designers and marketing in the research process.
  - IKEA has developed a retailing concept so unique (restaurant, play area, display, service, carry-out, marketing) that no other furniture or accessory competitor can match. They've identified customers' needs for convenience, variety, reasonable cost, and entertainment—all of which IKEA provides.
- *Suki o mitsukero*—Identifying a weakness or opportunity and taking advantage. Televised home shopping leader QVC Network studied competitor Home Shopping Network and identified two things that customers wanted: (1) Single or multihour product theme programs (Western jewelry, Irish crafts, Joan Rivers fashions, etc.) instead of offering a hodge-podge of items; and (2) The ability to order a product anytime once it had appeared on television. This close-to-the customer flanking strategy has made QVC Network the largest and most profitable television retailer to date.

A samurai maxim, taken from ancient Chinese strategist Sun Tzu and analogous to understanding both customers and the marketplace, goes[4]

If you know your opponent and you know yourself,
    you will always win;
If you don't know your opponent, but you know yourself,
    you will win only half the time.

> If you know neither your opponent nor yourself,
>   you will always lose.

In other words, don't allow gaps to form between provider and customer; and, if a competitor has allowed a gap to exist, the alert customer-driven company will be in a position to take advantage of it.

A related maxim speaks directly to being close to changing customer needs and expectations: "Expect nothing; be prepared for anything." Again, the proactive provider not only keeps an eye on the customer and marketplace, the same provider uses this information to offer customers products and services beyond expectations. Above all, the provider stays close enough to the customer that perceptual gaps cannot develop.

Product and Service Transactions: The Concept of *Touch*

Product and service transactions are those elements and components of performance need and expectation attributes (time, reliability) that bring the customer in direct contact with delivery and delivery staff. They are also called *critical incidents* or, as defined by Jan Carlzon of Scandinavian Airlines, *moments of truth.*

It is in these transactions, and how they are experienced by customers and providers, that the greatest opportunities for perceptual gaps can occur. Earlier, we identified types of direct customer-provider contact as the level of touch. As an example, when a customer is using direct response for purchase, such as catalogs or infomercials, there is generally low touch, or little or no direct contact between the provider and customer. Needs and performance are fairly straightforward. Lands' End, an outstanding direct marketer of clothing and equipment, recognizes its customers' need for trust in the value and quality of products and the people who provide them. In direct response purchase situations, the people are never seen. Lands' End sends each new customer a brochure featuring pictures of their staff (close to 200) in factory, office, and home settings. The brochure also contains Lands' End's business principles. The net effect is an increase in confidence and trust in the company, creating proactive touch in an industry where there is otherwise little or none.

Amica Insurance, one of the most efficient and service-oriented direct marketing insurers in the United States, turns low touch into a positive for policyholders and prospects. In a life insurance brochure entitled "Information not Interruptions," they say

> When you're at home relaxing, one of the last things you may want is to be interrupted by a life insurance agent. At Amica Life, we understand.

We're different.

We understand that Amica Policyholders are well informed individuals, capable of making important buying decisions without pressure from a sales person.[5]

As stated by Amica's chairman, Joel N. Tobey, in their 1993 Annual Report: "Few companies can match the level of attention we provide our policyholders—and we intend to keep it that way."[6]

At the other end of the touch spectrum is health care, where, in a hospital, a patient comes in contact with admissions staff, nurses, doctors, food service personnel, volunteers, technicians, and many others. Pacificare, a leading group-model managed care corporation based in California, has recognized that members who are pleased with their medical services, particularly those provided by their primary care physicians, will both remain with Pacificare and encourage friends, coworkers, and others to join. Studies conducted by Pacificare during the mid-1980s to understand member needs found that a high level of professional competence was assumed, and that it was not a differentiator between plans. According to Roger Taylor, M.D., executive vice president of Pacificare, the real difference between medical staffs—and, by extension, between medical plans—was the amount of touch, or personal consideration, compassion, and communication offered.

When people are ill, or have some type of medical condition, Pacificare learned their principal need is to be taken care of, to be nurtured. This is a requirement of both their health provider and plan, and it translates to the quality of care and service. The two basic levels of Maslow's need hierarchy cover these physical and safety needs. In 1986, Pacificare initiated a collaborative training program with their physician groups to be more sensitive to those needs. Called "The Art of Caring," the program's objectives are to have Pacificare's medical professionals demonstrate a cooperative, helpful, and respectful attitude toward patients and their families. It includes the training of providers and their staff in many visually and orally reinforcing behaviors. Some of these are

- Calling patients by name
- Asking patients questions about their treatment
- Speaking slowly and listening
- Sitting down and in proximity to the patient
- Explaining their treatment plan in simple terms

For physicians and their staffs, the concept of touch even extends to nonverbal, physical contact between them and their patients—holding their hands, touching their shoulders, and so on. This program has, in all respects, yielded impressive results. In purely business terms, it helped Pacificare maintain one of the industry's highest member retention levels. Members rate Pacificare's performance very highly. Members have also stayed with their primary care physicians with greater frequency. The rate of member complaints has declined dramatically.

The physicians themselves are enthusiastic about the program. They can see the positive results of training in their patient relations, and they have been impressed that Pacificare would offer such a proactive approach to members.[7] Providing customers with a higher, more responsive level of touch, in other words, has greatly contributed to Pacificare's success.

The interrelationship of needs and transactions in consumer industries like health care, food service, finance, lodging, entertainment, gaming, air travel, and most business-to-business situations is likely to be complex. The complexity in business-to-business markets extends to the purchase decisions themselves. Purchases are frequently for large dollar amounts and over sustained periods. They may require multiple decision makers and decision influencers, negotiation, detailed specifications, and a depth of knowledge by both customer and suppliers. The nature of these decisions requires that suppliers develop high touch, or close working relationships and customized service, with their customers.

Key Risk Management Services (KRMS) is a workers' compensation insurer, providing employee coverage through their customers—several thousand employers in North Carolina. Functioning through not-for-profit employer associations and insurance agencies, KRMS has an impressive record of client retention, offering an equally impressive and thorough array of services.[8]

- Loss control—returning employees to work at an early point, and drug testing to reduce workplace accidents
- Aggressive claims management—close monitoring of employees' cases
- Medical case management—maximizing employees' medical improvement to return employees to work and reduce the amount of the claims, lost productivity, and retaining expense
- Network of medical providers—saving employers money and ensuring immediate treatment in a controlled claims environment
- Pharmacy network—offering savings on most medications
- Education training and development—offering free safety seminars offered around the state and safety videos to reduce workplace accidents

- Continuous underwriting—providing special services to employers with higher workplace accident rates
- Customer services—supporting and assisting employers through publications, claims tracking, and resolution of problems

When employers in the associations are considering workers' compensation coverage, they are making complex cost and service-based decisions. Competition in this arena is challenging, but KRMS has studied the specific needs and transactional components of their customers, and offered services based on that knowledge and experience. They touch customers through programs like the education seminars and videos and proactive customer service, making information and support highly accessible.

Some industries tend to concentrate more on transaction assessment than evaluating performance characteristics or attributes. This is especially true where high customer touch is involved.

Examples of Perceptual Gap

Potential for perceptual gap can occur any time service providers misinterpret or fail to gauge the effect or impact of their delivery on a customer, in other words, don't take into account customer expectations and then respond accordingly. Consider these examples.

- A discount hardware and home products chain provided excellent prices and stock coverage, but its retailing approach called for few floor personnel. Management believed that prices and stock were more important than service until a competitor moved into its markets offering competitive pricing and stock coverage, *and* having well-trained, plentiful staff to serve customers. By the time management had understood this gap, they'd been dealt a severe customer loss.
- A chemical products company was occasionally in short supply of some stock items, and, when that occurred, it was forced to put some of its midsized and smaller accounts on allocation. Its sales representatives and sales managers received few complaints about this situation and so assumed customers were satisfied with product availability.

  A competitor guaranteed stock availability, and many of the small and medium-sized accounts, and some of the larger ones, switched to that company.
- The supplier of technical software had multiyear contracts with customers and sent out frequent programming updates, which

required its customers to invest technicians' time to make sure they were running current versions of the software. The company had relatively few sales representatives and relied on an 800 line for inquiries and complaints. It received few calls and so assumed the programming changes were being well received and that customers were continuing to update; however, many customers were so frustrated by update complexities, they discontinued or scaled back use of the software and were uncertain about renewing their contracts.

When a competitor offered easier programming and more field service support, many customers defected.

- A regional fast food company endeavored to compete with the major national chains by providing a better experience and better value to customers. The company used customer comment cards at every table, and its customers gave it high marks on satisfaction. Field staff management was equally positive.

   When sales begin to flag, senior management dispatched a small army of mystery shoppers to better understand what was happening. In comparison to competitors, the mystery shopper research revealed slow service, dirty stores, curt and unmotivated personnel, and cold food. Further, the drive-through service, which the company had not even tried to research, was particularly bad, that is, slow service, incorrect orders, and mischarges.

   While employing this information to make major service improvements, senior management also decided to conduct a full-scale telephone research project among both current and former customers. They found that their current customers had a low level of loyalty to the company—contrary to the findings from the customer comment cards—and that many of the former customers had left for precisely the reasons uncovered by the mystery shoppers.

- Sales representatives, sales managers, and service personnel at one automotive company's dealerships paid a lot of attention to owners for the first year or so as a result of incentive contests and quality checks; however, they lost touch and interest over time. Four or five years later, when these buyers were reentering the market, they exhibited little loyalty to the brand or dealership.

   It should be noted that newer franchises, particularly Saturn, Lexus, and Infiniti, have taken proactive steps to be close to their customers. Throughout the life of ownership, these companies have made sure that they regularly communicate with

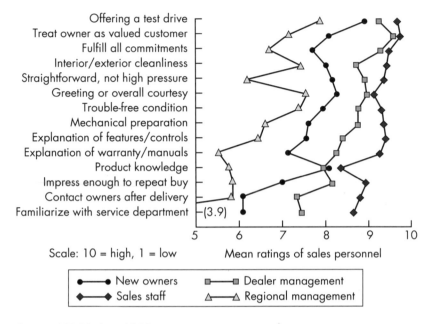

Offering a test drive
Treat owner as valued customer
Fulfill all commitments
Interior/exterior cleanliness
Straightforward, not high pressure
Greeting or overall courtesy
Trouble-free condition
Mechanical preparation
Explanation of features/controls
Explanation of warranty/manuals
Product knowledge
Impress enough to repeat buy
Contact owners after delivery
Familiarize with service department ⊢(3.9)

Scale: 10 = high, 1 = low   Mean ratings of sales personnel

| ●——● New owners | ■——■ Dealer management |
| ◆——◆ Sales staff | △——△ Regional management |

Source: ARBOR, Inc., 1991.

Figure 6.1. Customer-provider gaps, Western region.

customers, and their sales and service staffs are trained accordingly.

Figure 6.1 shows an example of a region where dealership sales representatives and dealership owners/managers and regional staff were dramatically out of alignment with new car owners. Several of these gaps were found to be directly related to owner attrition and defection.

Prescriptions for Narrowing or Eliminating Customer-Provider Perceptual Gaps

Just as there are many ways for customers and providers to misalign, thus creating perceptual gaps, there are also methods of narrowing or eliminating gaps.

Assessment

What information do you currently have about customers and their perceptions? How well does what customers tell you correlate with your company's cultural readiness for customer focus? In *Thriving on*

Chaos, Tom Peters advised companies to reengineer themselves into organized customer responsive enterprises and "launch a customer revolution."[9] This requires an adaptive culture; senior management commitment; well-trained, capable staff; and a nonstop flow of customer input. It also includes regular staff input as part of the process.

Proactive Service

Proaction is simple. The concept asks only that companies actively and continuously listen to customers so that they can be ahead of the curve on customer needs. Office products retailer Office Max, for example, stays ahead of customers' needs for saving time and making informed purchases by providing a product catalog, service desk, knowledgeable staff, and an innovative product card system.

Gather and Understand Needs

Spot-checking customer opinions and getting satisfaction report cards provides little value or direction and has minimal impact on corporate culture. Companies require a strategic approach to customer-defined needs, expectations, and problems. They should include both current *and* former customers in the process. They should provide hands-on training for staff so they can participate in capturing the customers' voice.

Identify Areas of Latent and Registered Complaint

As discussed earlier, frequently companies don't provide adequate opportunities for customers to complain or don't recognize that many customers will discontinue or reduce patronage without telling you why. Companies must identify and assess all areas of complaint.

Debrief Staff

Many companies conduct employee satisfaction studies, but fail to ask staff how they think customers feel about performance complaints, satisfaction, and loyalty. So, when customers' feedback is shared—particularly when it's negative—staff tends to disbelieve or discount it. Staff ought to participate in customer research as respondents, ideally completing the same questionnaire as customers, answering as they think customers would.

Deployment

Once customer and staff perceptual information is in hand, use it to identify areas of product or service improvement. Communicate it throughout the organization. Train cross-functional quality improvement teams.

Reinforce customer proaction and responsiveness skills. Plan for improvement programs and follow-up measurement.

√ *Empowerment*

Does your company provide enough flexibility and freedom of action for customer-facing staff to be proactive, to fix customer problems right away, to be customer advocates, to listen? Can managers do the same or are they too removed from customers? Staff should have both the authority *and* responsibility to work to customers' needs.

Several of these prescriptions will be covered in greater detail later in the book. They have been introduced in this chapter to allow readers to begin considering them.

Exercise

Branch managers and service staff at Twentieth Century National participate in the customer-retention survey process by completing the same questionnaires as the customers (definitely a sign that Twentieth Century wants both customer alignment and a cultural paradigm change).

Twentieth Century finds that, while tellers and customer service representatives align with customers on the importance and lack of availability of personal service, branch managers rate it low in importance and high in performance. Further, personal service is a key contributor to loyalty attrition and customer defection.

How should Twentieth Century address this situation? Think in terms of deployment and training (cross-functional with other bank service staff).

Summary

Customer-provider gaps exist because customers have one perception of the quality of product or service delivery and the organization has another. Having perceptual misalignment, or customer-provider gaps, is potentially harmful to customer loyalty. Remember that gaps can be a negative when they exist with customers, but a positive if they exist between competitors and their customers.

Transactions, or critical incidents, are the point at which customer and product, service, or provider meet; and they are frequently the cause of customer-provider gaps. Prescriptions for narrowing or eliminating customer-provider gaps include organizational/informational assessment, proaction, staff input, deployment, and empowerment.

Notes

1. *Ideals of the Samurai,* William Scott Wilson trans. (Burbank, Calif.: Ohara Publications, 1982), 115–16.

2. Valarie A. Zeithaml, A. Parasuraman, and Leonard L. Berry, *Delivering Quality Service* (New York: The Free Press, 1990), 38.

3. Thomas J. Peters and Robert H. Waterman, Jr., *In Search of Excellence* (New York: Warner Books, 1982), 13–15.

4. Philip Kotler, Liam Fahey, and S. Jatusripitak, *The New Competition* (Englewood Cliffs, N. J.: Prentice-Hall, 1985), 21.

5. Amica Life Insurance Company brochure, (Providence, R.I.: Amica Life Insurance Company, 1994).

6. Amica Insurance 1993 Annual Report (Providence, R.I.: Amica Life Insurance Company).

7. Dr. Roger Taylor, interview with author, July 1994.

8. Key Risk Management Services, Inc., promotional brochure, (Greensboro, N.C.: KRMS, 1994).

9. Tom Peters, *Thriving on Chaos* (New York: Alfred A. Knopf, 1988), 151–57.

Chapter 7

What Is the Competition Doing?

There is no greater misfortune than underestimating the enemy. If I underestimate the enemy, I am in danger of losing my fortune.[1]

—Lao Tzu, *Tao Te Ching*

Being better than the competition rarely means doing one thing vastly better. It usually means doing many little things just that little bit better. It is important, therefore, to know what your competitors are doing. . . . It makes sense to put your efforts into monitoring your competitors' performance in these areas.[2]

—Denis Walker, *Customer First*

Becoming Competitor-Oriented as Well as Customer-Driven

Most good marketing plans have a detailed section on competitive activity—strengths and weaknesses, new initiatives, and market penetration. Companies, large and small, can learn as much about product and customer service strategy from Schwarzkopf, Patton, Von Clausewitz, Napoleon, Genghis Khan, Theodoric, Julius Caesar, Alexander, and Sun Tzu as they do from observing industry leaders. At the same time they are addressing customer issues, they must also look at competition and plan accordingly.

In *Corporate Combat*, author William Peacock has identified a number of well-known examples where one corporation has used market knowledge and awareness of customer needs to gain a competitive advantage over another, including

- *Hallmark vs. American Greetings Corporation*—American Greetings, with more innovative but less expensive greeting cards than Hallmark, wanted to improve its market position. The company elected to gain attention, and, hopefully, increased market share, by developing the Strawberry

Shortcake novelty doll. It was broadly licensed, and American Greetings expanded its market coverage to department stores. By 1984 (When Peacock's book was written), American Greetings rose to almost 30 percent of market share while Hallmark, which made its own market countermoves, still lost 17 share points.

- *Seiko vs. other watch manufacturers*—When Seiko (the Japanese word for *precision*) entered the watch marketplace, it concentrated on middle price ranges and unique designs—the digital look, the calculator look, and chronographs. This was an area of the market that was weak for most other competitors. They used the design, production, and distribution advantages they had to compete with lower-priced and higher-priced watches. Within less then a decade, Seiko had more than half of the U.S. watch market.

- *The Beetle vs. the big three*—When Volkswagen entered the U.S. market in the '50s it had interesting features (air-cooled rear placement engine, reliability, and economy) but several disadvantages (small size, lack of power, and difficulty of servicing). In addition, it followed the unsuccessful market introduction of the similarly compact Nash Rambler. Volkswagen met these issues directly by dealing with specific customer needs, expectations, and problems. Its major strategy was to offer buyers a service warranty and contract, now common, but unknown at the time.[3]

Strategizing Services Relative to Competition

Al Ries and Jack Trout, writing in *Marketing Warfare*, suggest four ways a company can get closer to customers and position its delivery strategy relative to competition.

1. *Defense.* Companies with market dominance (leaders) should defend against competitors. Nonleaders should not consider it. American Express was able to do this with its "membership has it privileges" campaign, which built the desire of social acceptance by cardholders around an already strong position.

   Attack the company's own position. Introduce new products or services that improve marketplace strength. Some large HMOs, for example, have begun to offer their versions of traditional indemnity programs to leverage their attraction to employers and health care customers.

Leaders should always block competitive strategies. Wal-mart, now the country's largest retailer, has been able to blunt Kmart's price club aspirations with broader marketplace coverage and greater anticipation of customer needs.

2. *Offense.* Companies that are not market leaders, but still strong, can mount offensive approaches. If there are several commercial printers in a market, one dominant and the others active and competitive, any (or all) of them can develop offensive service strategies designed to challenge the market leader. They might do it with longer hours or greater varieties of paper in stock. If they find unmet customer needs, these needs may represent a weakness in the leader's position, such as price, quality, reliability, or service.

   Focus on a single or narrow area of attack. Swordmaster Miyamoto Musashi called this strategy "striking at the corners." If it is learned that the market leader has several areas of competitive vulnerability, concentrate resources on one area. If the leader moves to defend, this may open up other possibilities. Volkswagen used service guarantees to build its franchise, then later used the Beetle's design simplicity and dealer coverage to defend it. Federal Express competed with (then) larger airfreight carriers almost exclusively on overnight delivery service using its unique Memphis hub system.

3. *Flanking.* This is a risky move, with potentially big rewards, to gain advantages. It requires both competitive information and customer need determination and market insight to identify segments or niches where opportunity exists. Successful companies include the Franklin Mint for limited edition collectibles; Volvo for safety-driven car buyers; "800 FLOWERS" for floral gift packages ordered by telephone; Samuel Adams for small batch beer; Haagen-Dazs for ice cream; and Healthy Choice for food products.

   Where possible, surprise should be used, since this offers the competitive advantage of time and resource conservation. Time, as military strategists will concur, is almost always on the side of the competitor with greater customer knowledge.

4. *Guerilla warfare.* This is the development of several or many tactical advantages that (especially) small companies can use to keep constant pressure on competitors. Extended hours, more service personnel, product innovations, price benefits, and short turn-around delivery service are just some of the tactics that can be used. Although more limited in resources, smaller

companies with in-depth understanding of customer needs are frequently able to try a second, third, or fourth tactic if the first doesn't work. As Mao Tse-Tung said in describing his engagement tactics: "The enemy advances, we retreat. The enemy camps, we harass. The enemy tires, we attack. The enemy retreats, we pursue." This, again, also applies the Japanese concept of suki, in which a competitor presents a gap, opening, weakness, or opportunity to seize.[4]

Developing Competitive Information

Critical to any competitive strategy or tactic, just as in the overarching goal of keeping customers, is information. None of the strategies or tactics presented will work effectively without current, detailed insights into the products, services, advertising, pricing, development, distribution, and operational specifics of key and emerging competitors. Information can be generated using one or several techniques. Each has its own level of actionability and validity. These include

1. "Blind" mail, telephone, or in-person studies among current customers, former customers, and competitors' customers. These customers can be identified through sales representatives' call records, other records such as customer data captured at point of sale, compilation company lists (business and professional names, tightly defined by geographic area), or through general public or business screening (using household lists or Yellow Pages).

   The greatest advantage of blind interviewing is that it produces objective data, since the company sponsoring the study is not revealed to respondents. If the sponsor is known, this could create a form of bias. Respondents may be overly kind in their evaluation if they are already positive toward the product or service, or they may use the opportunity to unload in the interview or on the questionnaire if they are negative. A competitor's customers may refuse to participate outright.

   Between the three approaches, mail carries considerably more jeopardy for a company as it analyzes the data. While relatively inexpensive (direct costs on a telephone study, for example, can be at least several times the cost of a mail study), response rates may be low (creating what research professionals call "nonresponse bias"); questionnaires may be filled out incompletely; exploratory or open-ended questions get little detail; and if the company had a specific order to the questions in mind, this cannot be controlled using mail. The largest concern in a mail survey, however, is lack of surety as to who completed it. If it went to a customer's purchasing agent, for instance, a secretary or a subordinate may have filled it out. To address some of these issues, there should be some professional telephone interviewing among customers who didn't respond to the mail so that results can be compared to mail-based data.

Telephone and personal interviews provide greater control and, as a result, more reliability than mail. While trained to respect the company's customers (and former and competitors' customers), skilled professional interviewers are also able to make sure that the questions are totally understood, that the interview is completed in full, and that open-ended opinion questions are covered to several levels of detail.

With this information in hand, companies are able to see and understand where there are performance differences between themselves and competitors (Gap Profiles) and where those differences represent competitive opportunity or vulnerability (Competitive Leverage Profiles).

Figure 7.1 and Figure 7.2 illustrate two ways of looking at the same competitive performance data. In Figure 7.1, the Gap Profile, it can be seen that the Retail Hardware Chain has higher performance than Competitor A on two attributes, lower performance on two attributes, and parity (though low) performance on two attributes. The specific performance attribute customer impact is central to the concept of customer loyalty, and this will be fully discussed in the next chapter.

The Competitive Leverage Profile (Figure 7.2) shows the same data, but in a way to give them added meaning. Here it can be seen that Retail Hardware Chain had potential competitive leverage (among its customers) relative to Competitor A on "products available during sales" and "stock a variety of products to meet my needs;" however, there was extreme potential vulnerability on service by floor personnel." (Note: Usually any competitive score within ten percentage points of one another indicates performance parity.)

The word *potential* is used to describe both leverage and vulnerability. Potential would only be connected to actual leverage and vulnerability when and if it is determined that the advantage is actually helping to keep customers or the disadvantage is helping to lose them. This can be done through specialized analysis and modeling.

Company vs. competitors*

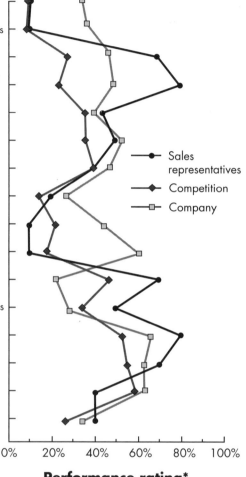

Representatives
Visibility of sales representatives

On-site availability of sales representatives

General product knowledge of sales representatives

Sales representatives inform us when new products are available

Customer service representatives resolve problems to our satisfaction

Service
Willingness of manufacturer to accept returns

Positive attitude when problems occur

Keep customers well-informed when product shortages occur

Availability
Product availability

Low incidence of product shortages

Price
Pricing

Willing to offer special prices to customers

Product Quality
Consistent product quality

Low incidence of product recalls

Other issues
Billing/invoicing accuracy

Ability to anticipate customers' needs

0%   20%   40%   60%   80%   100%

Performance rating*
*Based on percentage of high (5) ratings on a five point scale

Source: ARBOR, Inc., 1994.

Figure 7.1. Gap Profile.

2. Another way of looking at competitive performance is a modified version of mystery shopper called <u>competitive shopper</u>. Shoppers evaluate both the company and competitors on the same criteria, but are usually recruited by a third party (such as a market research supplier), so their assessments are objective. This technique has repeatedly proven effective in consumer

Comparative performance ratings

Representatives

1. Sales representative visibility
2. On-site availability
3. General product knowledge
4. Inform when new products available
5. Customer service representatives resolve problems to our satisfaction

Service

6. Willingness to accept returns
7. Positive attitude when problems occur
8. Keep customers well-informed when product problems occur

Availability

9. Product availability
10. Low incidence of product shortages

Price

11. Pricing
12. Willing to offer special prices to customers

Product Quality

13. Consistent product quality
14. Low incidence of product recalls

Other issues

15. Billing/invoicing accuracy
16. Ability to anticipate customer needs

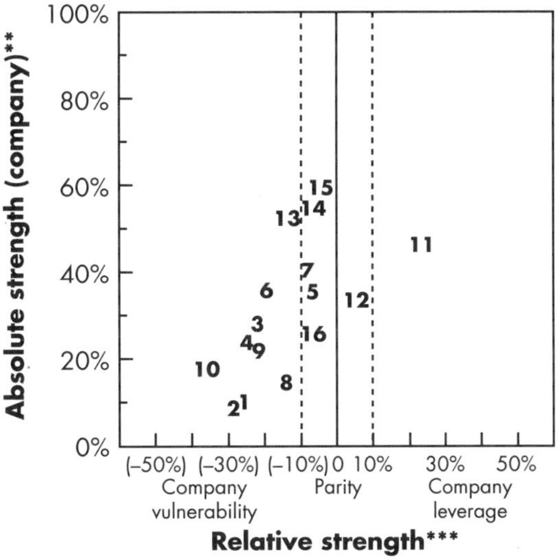

Source: ARBOR, Inc., 1994.

Figure 7.2. Competitive Leverage Profile.

goods and services, but has been used less frequently in business-to-business situations.

3. A third method of assessing competitive strengths and weaknesses is through direct observation on the competitive site or testing of the competitor's product. Companies deploy their staffs to see what the competition is doing. Observation in retail settings actively takes place. It's one way Burger King always knows what new programs McDonald's is launching, and vice versa.

In entering new markets in the United States and around the world, the Japanese raised observation and market intelligence to a fine science. Beginning over 40 years ago, Japanese trading companies (known originally as *zaibatsu*, now called *keiretsu*), their Ministry of Trade and Industry (MITI), and Japan External Trade Organization (JETRO) have regularly sent marketing executives and managers into markets to learn how a customer goes through the buying process. They might, for instance, observe women buying perfume and makeup in retail settings to identify what product features appeal to them.

They have also sent production and operations experts into factories to learn about the relationships of product development to customer needs and wants.

4. There are several other less traditional methods for companies to generate competitive information. These include publicly available industry or market studies, such as are conducted by the U.S. government or consulting firms (like Frost and Sullivan and the Stanford Research Institute), trade associations, trade publications, business and consumer press (using reference guides like Business Periodicals Index, the *Wall Street Journal* Index, the *New York Times* Index, Value Line, Dun and Bradstreet, Standard & Poors, *The Reader's Guide to Periodic Literature*), and information made available by companies themselves (10-k forms, prospectuses, annual reports).

Dimensions of Competitive Strategy

Professor Michael Porter has recognized the profound requirement for customer, industry, and self-knowledge companies must have in formulating competitive programs. He has identified 13 separate dimensions a company needs to consider in strategic planning.[5]

- *Specialization*—The degree to which it focuses its efforts in terms of the width of its line, the target customer segments, and the geographic markets served.
- *Brand identification*—The degree to which it seeks brand identification rather than competition based mainly on price or other variables. Brand identification can be achieved via advertising, sales force, or a variety of other means.
- *Push versus pull*—The degree to which it seeks to develop brand identification with the ultimate consumer directly versus the support of distribution channels in selling its product.
- *Channel selection*—The choice of distribution channels, from captive to mass.

- *Product quality*—Its level of product quality, in terms of raw materials, specifications, adherence to tolerances, features, and so on.
- *Technological leadership*—The degree to which it seeks technological leadership versus following or imitation. It is important to note that a firm could be a technological leader but deliberately not produce the highest quality product in the market; quality and technological leadership do not necessarily go together.
- *Vertical integration*—The extent of value added as reflected in the level of forward and backward integration adopted, including whether the firm has captive distribution, exclusive or owned retail outlets, an in-house service network, and so on.
- *Cost position*—The extent to which it seeks the low-cost position in manufacturing and distribution through investment in cost-minimizing facilities and equipment.
- *Service*—The degree to which it provides ancillary services with its product line, such as engineering assistance, an in-house service network, credit, and so forth. This aspect of strategy could be viewed as part of vertical integration, but is usefully separated for analytical purposes.
- *Price policy*—Its relative price position in the market. Price position usually will be related to other variables such as cost position and product quality, but price is a distinct strategic variable that must be treated separately.
- *Leverage*—The amount of financial leverage and operating leverage it bears.
- *Relationship with parent company*—Requirements on the behavior of the unit based on the relationship between a unit and its parent company. The firm could be a unit of a highly diversified conglomerate, one of a vertical chain of businesses, part of a cluster of related businesses in a general sector, a subsidiary of a foreign company, and so on. The nature of the relationship with the parent will influence the objectives with which the firm is managed, the resources available to it, and perhaps determine some operations or functions that it shares with other units (with resulting cost implications).
- *Relationship to home and host government*—In international industries, this refers to the relationship the firm has developed or is subject to with its home government as well as host governments in foreign countries where it is operating. Home governments can provide resources or other assistance to the

firm, or, conversely, can regulate the firm or otherwise influence its goals. Host governments often play similar roles.

These dimensions must be equally applied to understanding competitors. Lacking competitor knowledge and the knowledge of competitive customers' needs, expectations, and problems is almost as great a challenge as not understanding the company's customers and its own strengths and weaknesses. As Robert Heller said in *The Supermanagers*,

> The evidence comes from deep and continuing study of the market and those competing in it. The Supermanager uses this knowledge in planning a competitive strategy that will avoid the opposition's points of maximum strength, but rather, by intelligent use of tactical means . . . will concentrate on outflanking the enemy and hitting him where he is weakest. Above all, the starting position of fundamental realism is maintained, whatever happens.[6]

Exercise

A Twentieth Century National bank manager in one of your smaller operating regions reports that a new bank, Flagship State Bank, has just opened up near a small strip shopping center on the outskirts of a medium-sized, medium-income suburban village. Twentieth Century has four branches, each within three miles of Flagship, and they have all lost customers to Flagship. What importance does this have to Twentieth Century National? What can you do to learn about this competitor? What strategies or tactics might you initiate?

Summary

Companies must become competitor-oriented as well as customer-oriented, recognizing that strategy will be dependent on their own position within the marketplace. Competitive information, especially from customers, will help formulate the strategy. Observation and published customer and competitive data may also be helpful.

There are a number of specific dimensions companies must consider in planning strategy. These include customer, marketing, technical, organizational, and financial components. The dimensions apply to analyzing competition as well.

Notes

1. Lao Tzu, *Tao Te Ching* (Richard Wilhelm edition) (London, Arkana: 1978), Part II (DE), 59.

2. Denis Walker, *Customer First* (Brookfield, Vt.: Gower, 1990), 15.

3. Examples drawn from William E. Peacock, *Corporate Combat* (New York: Facts On File, 1984).

4. Ideas drawn from Al Ries and Jack Trout, *Marketing Warfare* (New York: McGraw-Hill, 1986).

5. Michael E. Porter, *Competitive Strategy: Techniques for Analyzing Industries and Competitors* (New York: The Free Press, 1980).

6. Robert Heller, *The Supermanagers* (New York: McGraw-Hill, 1984), 21.

Planning for Research, Developing Research Instruments, and Meaningfully Reporting Customer Service Research Results

Three times a year one should have an able and honest retainer go around the province, listen to the opinions of the four classes of people (samurai, farmers, artisans and merchants) and devise some policy in regard to those opinions.[1]

—Asakura Toshikage, Daimyo of Echizen, (1428–1481 A.D.)

You won't discover how you're doing on the majority of characteristics that mean most to customers unless you develop a reliable method for learning customers' opinions.[2]

—Richard C. Whiteley, *The Customer-Driven Company*

From the unreal lead me to the real! From darkness lead me to the light![3]

—Swami Nikhilananda, *The Upanishads*

Who, What, When, and How

Who

Who refers to who actually conducts the customer research—the company or an outside research firm. While it is valuable to have a cross-functional team actively participate in qualitatively gathering customer need, problem, expectation, and complaint information, generally speaking it is not cost-effective or time-effective to have the company itself conduct quantitative customer research, that is, interviews and analysis. Also, there is the possibility that bias could enter either data collection or interpretation.

Customer research firms can support companies at both qualitative and quantitative phases, often providing unique methods of evaluating data (see chapter 9). Some companies, such as Goodyear and MBNA, conduct so much customer-related research, they have found it more beneficial to operationally control the complete customer research system from inside.

Who also refers to the appropriate customer to be interviewed. Is it the decision maker (such as a customer's officer), a decision influencer (such as a design engineer), or a liaison (such as a purchasing agent)? These may each be segments of the customer population, so any or all of them could be interviewed.

What

The information included in the customer measurement system is all-important. Some recommendations are in the next section.

When

Companies should decide how often to formally debrief customers—continuously, weekly, monthly, quarterly, semiannually, annually, or less. If there are no strictly mandated data collection frequency guidelines or rules (such as by an industry trade group), companies will determine this by

- Marketplace changes/dynamics
- Level/intensity of competition
- Their own ability to deploy/act on findings

When also means when to collect information during the year. As a rule, it is somewhat more difficult to generate information from consumers or industrial customers over the summer, during vacation time, and around the Thanksgiving, Christmas, and New Year holidays. Any other time of the year is satisfactory.

How

As discussed elsewhere in the book, there is a hierarchy of field method preference for how to conduct customer research.

- Personal interviews
- Telephone interviews
- Mail/self completion interviews

Just as for qualitative research, conducting customer interviews in-person absolutely ensures that the correct person is being interviewed, that all of the questions are being answered (unless the customer expresses a desire not to answer), and that in-depth verbatim and anecdotal responses are obtained. It can be a prohibitively expensive technique, however, and especially for industrial customers, sometimes difficult to obtain cooperation or schedule appointments.

Mail or self-completion research is the least desirable technique because of a lack of surety that the correct person is completing the questionnaire, lack of control over the order of questionnaire completion, and the minute amount and superficial level of verbatim information generated. Also, mail-back research is subject to fairly low response rates, making validity suspect. Most targeted customers simply discard the questionnaire, and those who do respond often have an "agenda" and tend to be more negative than other customers. So, even though mail is far less expensive than other techniques, the likelihood of drawing incorrect conclusions and initiating change or training based on them (to which scarce company resources will be applied) is higher.

Telephone interviewing is perhaps the best alternative for conducting consumer or industrial research. Identification, control, and completion problems are greatly reduced. Some industrial companies have dissuaded their employees from participating in telephone or personal research, partially because they have not seen benefits from their suppliers' satisfaction-based approaches; however, skilled, respectful interviewers are adept at gaining cooperation and completion. Companies can also help their own situation with customers by sharing what they have learned in the research.

Another *how* issue is whether to identify the company as the sponsor of the research. As a guideline, what the company may lose in customer cooperation level because of disclosure frequently will be more than offset by keeping data collection as objective as possible by not revealing the company name. Customers often have positive or negative baggage, that is, opinions, regarding their suppliers, and it is more valuable to have that come through with a minimum of bias. Also, nondisclosure allows collection of competitive supplier data on the same footing within the same interview.

Keep It Simple and Begin at the Beginning

Professional market researchers consider themselves the experts on questionnaire and data evaluation construction, and indeed many are quite proficient at design, analysis, and reporting. However, just as expert attorneys can differ on the interpretation of law and expert physicians can differ on treatment of a patient, so there are many ways to construct a customer questionnaire that will produce retention-oriented information and reports that will best present it.

My purpose is not to anoint readers with instant market research capability, but rather to provide simple design and presentation guidelines. Although the research purist may debate exactly what is to be included in a customer measurement system (this is not a market research text), the following is suggested.

- Questionnaires
  - Qualification (screening) questions
  - Attribute importance
  - Attribute performance
  - Key transaction importance
  - Key transaction performance
  - Complaint question battery
  - Expectation (dimensional) questions
  - Overall performance questions
  - Best features/features needing improvement
  - Particular interest questions
  - Loyalty questions
  - Recommendation questions
  - Concept (optional) questions
  - Demographics
- Analytical plan
- Data reporting
  - Conclusions and implications of the findings (and deployment recommendations)
  - Summary of findings
  - Discussion of findings
  - Background and objectives
  - Method of study
  - Detailed tabular material/appendix
- Special analyses

This, with variation as needed, can form the basis of the system. Companies can look at these formats and decide if more simplicity or more detail are needed.

Questionnaires

Again, because this is not an academic text on market research and questionnaire or question construction (there are plenty of those already in the library), this book concentrates on question areas.

Qualification (Screening) Questions

If questionnaires are sent (via mail) to current customers, former customers, or competitors' customers, the company conducting the measurement can only hope that the individual receiving and completing the instrument is the correct person in the correct function. Usually, an introductory letter or even a telephone call (or fax) of some sort accompanies mail questionnaires, and this can help ensure that the questionnaires get to the correct individuals.

If interviews are to be conducted over the telephone, or if an appointment is being made to conduct it in person, screening confirms that the correct person is reached.

Depending on the type of customer, screening can be simple or complex. For example, if a consumer service company wishes to segment its customers according to frequency of service usage (perhaps only desiring to interview light users, heavy users, or recent users), this needs to be identified at the beginning of the interview.

Attribute Importance

Customer needs, expectations, problems, and complaints should have been determined by means of qualitative research, hands-on interviewing or a quantitative device such as the Van Westendorp technique (see chapters 4 and 5). Needs and expectations have been distilled into product, service, or image-type attributes for the research instrument. As previously discussed, they should be as operationally specific as possible.

For each attribute, customers are asked to rate its importance. Several methods can be used for ratings. My recommendation is presented in some detail in the next chapter, along with the rationale for asking attribute importance questions in the first place. Suffice it to say that importance is the customers' opportunity to attach a value to performance attributes and is one way the company can assign weights to these when prioritizing process improvement programs.

Attribute Performance

Attribute performance rating questions are at the core of any customer measurement system. The rating scale should neither be too simple or dichotomous (yes/no, excellent/poor), nor too detailed (scales much over ten points) for the customer to understand. Simplicity will be an impediment to actionability, since most every product or service attribute will have more gradations of performance than black/white. Overly detailed scales make it difficult for the customer to interpret, thus rendering it limited in applicability. Sometimes agree/disagree scales are used, but they require customers to have set feelings about an attribute when this may not be the case. Generally anchored, odd-numbered scales (5 point and 7 point) are preferred because they allow respondents to have neutral positions, if they feel this way. This provides sufficient sensitivity for analysis and for action.

Key Transaction Importance/Performance

Transactions or critical incident performance and importance can be rated like attributes. The challenge for companies incorporating transactions into the measurement system is that they be real *transactions* rather than attributes. For example, a typical performance attribute would be "friendliness of customer service staff," while a related transaction would be "customer service staff regularly addresses me by name when I call." Transactions can be especially directional when the service relationship is infrequent but considered important by the customer.

Complaint Question Battery

The intent of having complaint questions within the measurement system is threefold: (1) to quantitatively identify the array of issues, small and large, requiring attention; (2) to use the system as a triggering mechanism for action; and (3) to provide the basis for determining which expressed and unexpressed complaints relate to perceived overall performance and customer loyalty.

As previously discussed, complaint question batteries begin with totally open-ended or limited-scope (returned shipments, calls to customer service) complaint questions, also identifying whether the complaint has been registered with the company. If brought to the company's attention, there is a question dealing with the level of company action/resolution and the acceptability of that resolution.

If the complaint hasn't been brought to the company's attention, there is a question to determine the reason this was not done. Should the customer identify insufficient service hours, difficulty of finding/reaching sales or service staff, or unresponsive customer service, this is valuable input and comment on customer voice processes.

Finally, if the complaint was unregistered, or registered but not resolved, the battery includes asking the customer whether communication from the company is now desired. This is an opportunity for the company to be more proactive in dealing with complaints.

Expectation (dimensional) Questions

If the company has determined the optimal level of performance expectation on issues like time, volume, accuracy, and the like (see chapter 5 for detailed explanation), these can be measured with rating or agree-disagree scales. This is a quantitative verification of expectation levels.

When specific expectations haven't been identified prior to the formal, quantitative customer performance measurement program, this can still be done using a device known as split test or split run. It works this way. The company is trying to determine if the speed of customer service staff response to inquiries has an impact on loyalty. The current average call-back speed is 20 minutes. It could, if desired by customers, lower that time to 10 minutes, but it would mean increasing the size of customer service staff. On the other hand, if a call-back of 30 minutes has no impact on customer loyalty (even if customers are less satisfied), the company could reduce service staff.

Split runs deal with alternative expectation levels by equally dividing customer samples in the research so that they are considering the acceptability of only one dimensional level. Thus, in our example, equal samples of one-third of the customers included in measurement would assess call-back speeds of 10, 20, and 30 minutes.

Attributes Performed Best/Attributes Most Needing Improvement

At this point in the questionnaire, customers are asked to identify which attribute or attributes are performed best by the company and which are most in need of improvement. They then give their verbatim, or open-ended, reasons for these evaluations. These questions provide valuable input. Not only is it the customers' opportunity to voice reasons for positive or negative company performance, but the company is given additional direction as to improvement priority (for negatives) and marketing or communications opportunity (for positives).

Just as best/poorest performance attribute feedback can be generated, so can feedback on best/poorest critical incident. Attributes and critical incidents can even be prioritized as to performance, but this is generally a more challenging and time-consuming task for customers.

Particular Interest Questions

Some areas of product or service performance delivery benefit from additional closed (ratings or agree/disagree) or verbatim (open-ended) questions. These may cover current company or market situations—such as stock-outs, customer service hours, product returns, new product introductions, or sales staff turnover—when the company feels it could have some competitive exposure or opportunity.

Overall Performance/Loyalty/Recommendation Questions

Overall Performance. Customers are typically asked to evaluate companies in some overall manner. This is done either once, considering all areas of product/service delivery, or there may be multiple overall questions, each at the conclusion of an attribute or transaction section such as sales, shipment, billing, product performance, and customer service attribute sections.

Most frequently, these questions are phrased in a manner similar to, "How satisfied are you with (the company's) overall performance on _____?" Less often, the phrasing is similar to "Please rate (the company's) overall performance on _____." As discussed, satisfaction level may not be as actionable because of its passivity, so a direct overall performance rating or assessment will give more meaningful direction. Even so, using summary assessment questions can have some jeopardy. As stated by Susan Devlin and H. K. Dong of Bellcore, because service dimensions are multiple, "asking a customer to give only a single appraisal of either a specific service experience or the service provider in general—that is, the composite of many specific experiences—can be invalid as well as frustrating to the respondent."[4] As mentioned earlier, companies should not skimp on asking attribute and transaction questions.

The overall performance question may have a follow-up verbatim element that allows the customer to provide a reason for the rating.

Loyalty. Loyalty questions are absolutely essential if the company is to identify customers' motivations to continue its relationship with the company. They may be expressed as "How likely are you to continue purchasing from (company)?" or "How likely are you to remain a customer of (company)?

Dimensional levels can also be included in the question, as needed by the company. For instance, the company may wish to know if the customer expects to continue the relationship over *time* (for example, three months, six months, one year, and so on), or the amount of purchase or service *volume* (more, same, or less). If a former customer, the company may wish to determine likelihood of repurchase (timetable and amount).

Recommendation. The customer, whether an end consumer, design engineer, or purchasing agent, develops firm opinions about the company's products or services. Willingness to recommend, in addition to loyalty, is another powerful reflection of the strength of that opinion. The question "How likely are you to recommend (the company's) products/services to a friend or colleague?" is valuable because it demonstrates the degree of trust the customer has in staking or attaching reputation to company performance. As such, it should be considered almost as valuable as overall performance or loyalty questions.

Concept (optional) Questions

Often, companies have been considering new products or services or seen reactions to competitive products or services in the marketplace. In addition, in the qualitative, or needs identification, phase of the measurement system, some potentially new performance attributes, product or service concepts, or emerging issues may have arisen for which the company would now like to generate some quantitative and/or verbatim input. This is new information, not covered by the customer measurement system's core elements.

As examples, in needs identification research for clients, we have found situations such as

- New customer applications of a product (which would offer our client broader selling opportunities)
- Customer need for more descriptive and specific service information (service manuals)
- Response to new federal regulations regarding quality levels
- New products the company was adding to its line
- Service representative on-call availability in the evenings and on weekends
- Automatic product update information (quality reports, stock depth, delivery turnaround) to customers at regular intervals
- Special communication requirements of new customers
- Alternative shipping and billing schedules

Because customer needs are constantly evolving, customer measurement systems should be flexible enough to accommodate new or emerging opportunities. This information can then be correlated with overall performance or loyalty measures to gauge potential impact.

Demographics

How does the company wish to segment customers for marketing, sales, or service purposes? These are key resource allocation issues. In some instances, the company's own records will provide detailed information about customers—locations, volume, purchase frequency, and type of product purchased (purchase trends, specific market application). This is generally true in commercial and industrial markets in which the company can keep detailed files on its customers, competitors, and markets.

For many consumer product and service markets, the companies often have less access to customer information that would help segment and target their marketing efforts. These segments might include gender, age, income, family composition, and occupation (also spouse's occupation) as well as frequency and level of product/service usage. Such segmented information might extend to what is known as psychographic profiling, that is, customer opinions about social and political issues, their hobbies, leisure activities, reading proclivities, and so on.

Analytical Plan

Before the company begins reporting customer information to its management and staff, it should first have a detailed plan as to how the reservoir of data will be massaged and analyzed. Like questionnaire design, analysis plans need not be complicated, but they should have enough specifics that the company can use data to help reach objectives, improve performance quality, and increase customer retention levels.

Plans (and decisions) should include

- Analysis of performance attributes and critical incidents—by high ratings, low ratings, or mean scores? Unless mean scores are specifically desired (such as, for continuity with previous customer research), showing data this way is usually less effective because mean scores tend to "wash out" the data or remove the drama from them.
- Relationship data—Complaints, new ideas, and so on, cross-tabulated against overall performance questions, loyalty, and recommendation questions.
- Data reduction—If there is a large number of performance attributes or product/service transactions in the measurement system (and some high service intensity businesses like health care, lodging, gaming, financial services, food service, industrial service, and travel can have many attributes or transactions), is there a way to reduce these to a more manageable level?

  There are multivariate techniques like cluster analysis and factor analysis that can be applied to show the level of relationship between attributes. If closely related, these attributes can be combined for further analysis.
- Modeling techniques to be applied.
- Reporting of verbatim comments—Most customer-measurement systems generate verbatim, or open-ended, customer

response at several points, such as an explanation of low attribute or transaction ratings, best/worst features, complaints, particular interest areas, new concepts, and so on.

For reports, these valuable data are best presented by grouping responses and giving examples. However, the system can also be made more robust by channeling customer verbatims to the appropriate individual or department as soon as they are received. This is an opportunity for rapid proaction with the customer.

Automobile manufacturers understand the value of immediately directing comments obtained from new car buyers back to the dealership, customer service, or other groups (such as design) for further action. Likewise, hospitals will quickly give verbatim service comments (food service, nursing, admissions, billing) from recently discharged patients in their measurement system to the departments for immediate attention.

The only potential danger of a flow of customer verbatims is overreaction. There is a tendency to "chase every rabbit," that is, to strongly respond to each negative verbatim rather than deal with them strategically over time. So the best advice is close management of verbatim flow.

Data Reporting

The objective of any report is to express the customer's voice, objectively and usefully, for all who oversee or implement improvements. Customer data, typically, have a message of opportunity, changing performance, and evolving customer requirements, and a report is the instrument by which this is communicated.

Although order of presentation may vary depending on company culture or the specific requirements of management, reports generally have the following basic components.

Conclusions and Implications of the Findings (and Deployment Recommendations)

This section, while usually only a few pages in length, presents the analyst's interpretation of data for the company. It identifies where the company has performance leverage or vulnerability on the attributes themselves and relative to competition. If performance trends are moving in certain directions, and this has implications for the company, it is presented here. If some customer segments perceive performance more positively or negatively, implications are reviewed in this section. The section may also contain some graphics, if they make the conclusions easier to understand.

Finally, this section will have the analyst's prioritized recommendations for change or improvement. This begins the process of review and deployment for the company, leading to higher customer loyalty levels.

Summary of Findings and Trends

The summary section encapsulates the most relevant findings of data analyzed. Each section—attributes, transactions, complaints, modeling, customer segment—has highlights presented here.

Discussion of Findings and Trends

This section presents the detailed results of customer research or customer information system findings, including all performance and importance attributes, transactions, and complaints. Findings are presented for customer segments, regions, time periods, and demographics, if included. The analyst also presents any support graphics (such as tables or visual models) and relevant customer verbatim comments.

Customer measurement system information often tells a story, that is, a consistent message of performance improvement, slackening, leverage, or vulnerability in one or more areas that impacts customers' perceptions of overall quality and their loyalty. When internal or frontline customers, such as sales representatives, store managers, or customer-service staff, are included as part of the measurement system, their degree of alignment with customers is also part of the story.

The plot of the story is what leads to drawn conclusions and recommendations for improvement. In one example, a failure to continue a full communications program with inactive customers was central to the breakdown of customer loyalty. In another instance, a consistent lack of stock depth on some key items meant, to customers, that their orders were not only incomplete but late; and delivery timing was critical to maintain their loyalty. A third situation involved lack of design flexibility due to inexperienced, newly trained field design staff. All three core performance situations were reflected in many other, related measures.

Background and Objectives

The purpose of customer measurement should always be stated in every report, in part because the measurement system is constructed on this foundation, and in part because it keeps all the data users honest. There is a tendency for company management to want measurement systems to be like a sink, collecting everything in the customer's kitchen. With a statement of objectives, collected and reported data have defined parameters; and the analyst is asked to evaluate the information and make recommendations within those parameters. Also, if changes—additions or deletions—were made in the system, this is the section to state it.

Method of Study

Reports should also describe the sample design—who was interviewed and when and how they were interviewed. All relevant detail—such as customer segments, and reporting periods—should be outlined here. Also, if other research methods (such as qualitative study) or data sources (such as secondary information or company information) are used, they should be cited in this section.

Detailed Tabular Material/Appendix

Full tabular results, discussion outlines, sets of customer verbatims, and questionnaires can be included in the report as an appendix or as a separate document.

Above all, it is up to the dexterous analyst, whether a staff member inside the company or a professional researcher from a research and/or quality consulting firm, to make sense of customer information. As stated by Professor Thomas V. Bonoma in *The Marketing Edge*

> Monitoring marketing research, like anything else in marketing, requires an intimacy with the tasks at hand that allows converting data offered by the environment into information useful to management, even when the systems in place to provide that information do not do so in the manner best suited for decision-making. Generally speaking, there are far too much data and not nearly enough information available.[5]

In other words, customer measurement systems can always be modified and upgraded to provide more actionable data. They should be, in fact, and on a continuous basis. Meaningfully and objectively reporting results, from the reams and reams of data the system produces, is critical to prioritizing activities and processes for customer retention.

Exercise

Twentieth Century National's competitive situation makes it essential that bank management and staff have more detailed performance information from customer segments, former customers, competitors' customers, and bank frontline staff. Based on instrument and report design recommendations in this chapter, (re) design Twentieth Century's customer measurement system.

Summary

Identify *who* conducts the customer research and *who* is interviewed, *what* is asked, *when* to conduct the research, and *how* it is to be conducted. Follow logical steps in designing questionnaires—cover attributes (performance/importance), transactions, complaints, best/worst features, overall performance, and demographics. Construct a thorough data analysis plan. Generate a report and format that allows the company to act on/prioritize improvement efforts, plus provides logical evaluation of the findings that led to conclusions.

Notes

1. *Ideals of the Samurai*, William Scott Wilson trans. (Burbank, Calif: Ohara Publications, 1982), 70.

2. Richard C. Whiteley, *The Customer-Driven Company* (Reading, Mass.: Addison-Wesley, 1991), 165.

3. Swami Nikhilananda, *The Upanishads* (New York: Harper & Row, 1964), 189.

4. Susan J. Devlin and H. K. Dong, "Service Quality from the Customer's Perspective," *Market Research* 6, no. 1 (1994): 5–13.

5. Thomas V. Bonoma, *The Marketing Edge* (New York: The Free Press, 1985), 143.

Chapter 9

Customer Retention Modeling

*Consumers rely heavily on their own human senses to arrive at per-
ceptions about quality. The resulting perceptions are obviously influ-
ential in consumers' decisions on what to buy. It therefore becomes
important for (industrial) companies to learn what those perceptions
are and, as far as possible, to discover the detailed cause-and-effect relationship between consumer perceptions and the decision to buy.*[1]

—J. M. Juran, *Juran on Planning for Quality*

*Current satisfaction measurement systems are simply not designed
to provide insight into how many customers stay loyal to the company and for how long.*[2]

—Frederick F. Reichheld, "Loyalty-Based Management,"
Harvard Business Review, March–April, 1993

*A cause of dissatisfaction that does not translate to market damage is
not as important as one that does.*[3]

John A. Goodman, Scott M. Broetzmann, and Colin Adamson,
"Ineffective—That's the Problem with Customer Satisfaction
Surveys," *Quality Progress,* May, 1992

Limits of Non-Retention-Based Models
and Data

As discussed earlier, virtually every company deals with scarce time,
money, staff, and facilities as an everyday fact of life. How effectively
limited resources are applied to improving products or services has a
major impact on success. Prioritizing customer needs must first take
place, and this will guide resource allocation.

What is the appropriate process for prioritizing customer needs?
Companies have used many approaches and techniques, from the
simple to those so complex they rival the alchemists' formulas for
making gold. Here are some of them, along with a review of their limitations.

- *Attribute and transaction priorities for improvement based on (low to high) performance in the measurement system and, also, trends in performance.* (See Table 9.1 and Figure 9.1, which show how these data are displayed in a table and in a graph.) These data are also frequently displayed using means or averages. (See Figure 9.2.)

    The principal limitation of using only performance or performance trend data as a basis for improvement is one of *relationship.* As discussed in an earlier chapter, if a company invests

Table 9.1. Performance data/trends in tabular form.

	1991	1992	1993	1992–1993 Trend
Reliability	43%	43%	45%	3%
Responsiveness	54%	58%	54%	–4%
Delivery services	63%	64%	59%	–5%
Complaint handling	25%	19%	15%	–4%
Technical capability	51%	57%	72%	15%
Telephone experience	46%	48%	47%	–1%
Scheduling flexibility	45%	49%	49%	0
Pricing	54%	56%	56%	0
Overall support	33%	63%	55%	–8%
Product quality	47%	53%	52%	–1%

Source: ARBOR, Inc., client studies, 1991–1993.

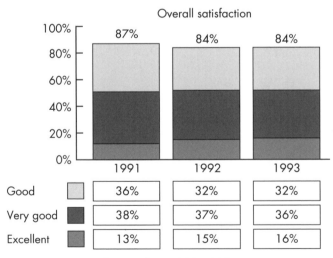

Source: ARBOR, Inc., client studies, 1991–1993.

Figure 9.1. Performance data/trends in graphic form.

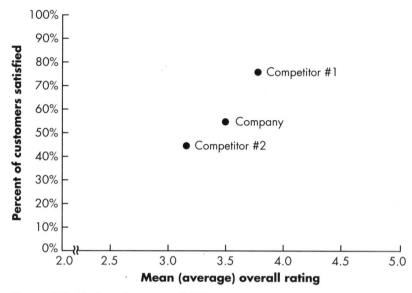

Source: ARBOR, Inc., client study, 1993.

Figure 9.2. Mean performance data in graphic form.

resources around low-scoring attributes, it may see little reward, either in increased satisfaction levels or, more importantly, higher customer loyalty rates. Performance results, used by themselves, don't relate to anything more actionable, like intention to purchase in the future.

Also, performance-only data assume that all attributes are equal in value. Any company whose measurement system includes attribute importance ratings as well as performance ratings knows that some attributes are definitely more important to customers than others.

Finally, measurement systems yielding models built around performance mean scores are depriving users of applicability. Here is a simple example. Assume five customers are rating Your Company's products or services for efficiency and accuracy attributes on a 10-point Likert scale, where 10 is excellent performance and 1 is poor performance. They are also rating Competitor A on the same attributes. Looking at their raw data and mean scores, we see the following:

All of them have the same mean scores, so if mean scores were the only thing being used for direction, the company wouldn't know what to do. The data have, in effect, been

	Efficiency		Accuracy	
	Your Company	Competitor A	Your Company	Competitor A
Customer 1	10	7	4	9
Customer 2	4	7	6	10
Customer 3	6	6	7	3
Customer 4	9	7	8	3
Customer 5	4	6	8	8
Mean score	6.6	6.6	6.6	6.6

washed out. We will discuss preferred approaches later in the chapter.

Some companies use discriminating power values in their modeling (the widest spread between high performance scores and low performance scores). Your Company has a discriminating value of 4 on accuracy (8 minus 4) compared to Competitor A, which has a discriminating value of 7 (10 minus 3). So what? Like mean scores, discriminating power values provide little direction.

- *Attributes and transactions prioritized based on their importance to customers.* This approach is subject to the same limitations as performance-only data; however, company customer measurement systems collect importance-only data far less frequently than performance-only question systems.

- *Analysis of former customers' attribute performance and importance scores.* Some companies are focused and fixated on customer loss to such an extent that they fail to recognize an attrition state on the part of current customers. It is extremely important to understand why current customers may be in the process of leaving. Customers in attrition will be more responsive to performance improvement than customers in a reclamation process.

- *Attribute and transaction performance benchmarked to competitive performance, perhaps even on (collective) mean scores compiled from multiple competitors.* Some companies also evaluate trends in their performance relative to competition. While benchmarking, as a performance criterion, shouldn't be undervalued, it nevertheless has some deficiencies as a basis for improvement. If all competing companies are performing marginally on a performance attribute or delivery transaction, does this represent a flanking or strategic opportunity or gap to be used to advantage? Or is it a performance attribute or delivery transaction that customers don't care much about? This must be determined before investing resources.

* *A formula-based Customer Satisfaction Index (CSI), Customer Satisfaction Quotient (CSQ), or other composite, single number approach.* These purport to be a key indicator of performance. (See Figure 9.3.) Sometimes, companies even use *index* as a replacement term for an overall quality or satisfaction score. Indices should always be viewed and used with some caution, for several reasons. First, and worst, like the alchemist's gold formula, they may represent so many attributes as to be almost impossible to understand. Second, closely related to complexity, they chain a company to a set of criteria. If the criteria change, or the weights assigned to criteria change, as

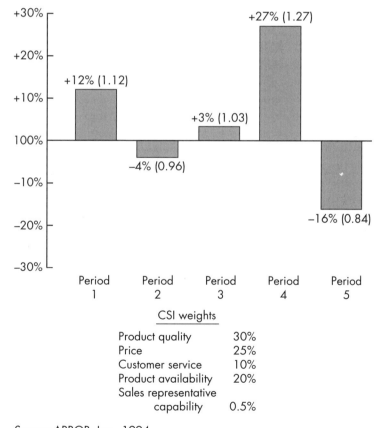

CSI weights	
Product quality	30%
Price	25%
Customer service	10%
Product availability	20%
Sales representative capability	0.5%

Source: ARBOR, Inc., 1994.

Figure 9.3. Customer satisfaction index example.

they inevitably must over time, the company is faced with re-computing back index data in a way that it won't compromise past survey results. Finally, a CSI can create "magic bullet-itis," a condition in which everyone in the company is totally focused on moving the CSI score ever upward. Salaries are tied to changing CSI results; careers are affected because of it. There have even been instances of customers being persuaded to rate companies in certain ways so that CSI scores can be manipulated and managed, rendering an already questionable approach almost worthless.

One diversified industrial products corporation has a partic-ularly elaborate method of developing and monitoring its CSIs. Working in partnership with customers, it develops an overall index that has close to 20 separate operational criteria (includ-ing reliability, inventory control, customer service, cost/value, and product development) of performance quality. The criteria have both qualitative and quantitative definitions. The criteria and definitions are reviewed annually. Customers can select a subset of these criteria that apply to their own company. While well-intended and customer-specific, this complex process makes it difficult for the corporation to get consistent, mean-ingful direction for improvement by customer segment.

- *Relationship models, such as importance based on multiple regression analysis, where the influence of each performance attribute on overall satisfaction rating is shown. (See Figure 9.4.)*

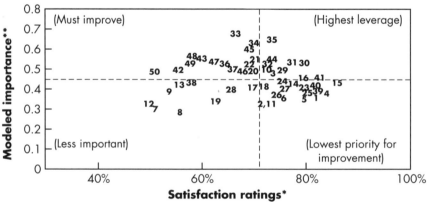

** Based on correlation with overall satisfaction rating

Source: ARBOR, Inc., 1994.

Figure 9.4. Relationship model.

Frequently, of course, these graphic and tabular data readouts reflect relationships to customer satisfaction, often, as shown in Figure 9.4, to an overall satisfaction rating or a CSI. As a consequence, though these displays of data often look impressive, they are minimally actionable. Or, if companies actively try to apply the findings, they may be disappointed with the result. The reason is that these models are built on a foundation of customer satisfaction, and, of course, satisfied customers are not necessarily loyal.

Customer Retention Modeling and the Mission of Customer Measurement

The mission of customer measurement is to (1) identify customer needs, expectations, problems, and complaints, (2) quantify them, and (3) use this information to offensively move the company to a state of customer-need anticipation, customer partnership, and customer loyalty.

If the measurement process is thought of as a hierarchy, customer retention modeling will be at or near the top. It is the vital link between customer data and stronger customer-provider relationships. In addition to overall actionability, loyalty modeling can reveal

- Where, and with what types of customers, the company is competitively at risk
- Where there are new business, new product, or new service opportunities
- Why customers buy, and why they buy from your company
- Where there are opportunities for lower costs or better communications
- Where customer needs are trending
- What problem areas require the most immediate response
- What customers' specific requirements and priorities are

With the related goals of minimizing customer attrition and defection and maximizing customer retention and loyalty, companies will derive the most value and direction from models that look at performance and importance *and* relate to customer loyalty. Both are important and contributory to company goals.

Three Integrated Models

We utilize three integrated models to help prioritize improvement, development, service, marketing, operations, planning, and communication activity.

- Customer Action Window^{SM}
- Dual Importance Window^{SM}
- Customer Motivation Window^{SM}

Each of these models includes measures of importance to customers. There is continuing discussion, even debate, over whether it is best to set up visual and mathematical models around measures of direct attribute importance (where the customer is asked, within the measurement system, to rate or attach a value to the importance of an attribute or delivery transaction) or modeled attribute importance (where the rating score given to a specific attribute is correlated to the score given to the rating of some overall measure of performance).

Those arguing in favor of direct importance ratings feel that customers can always identify what is important to them. Where customers are evaluating the importance of soft attributes, that is, those having to do with company image or customers' own feelings, this may not always be true. While several methods can be used to generate importance data—rank ordering attributes, constant sum—we tend to use verbally anchored scales, where customers can give a rating ranging from "not at all important" to "extremely important."

Those arguing against direct importance make two points.

- There is a tendency for there to be less dimensionality, that is, for customers to say that everything is important.
- Interpretation of the questions may be somewhat open, that is, all customers may not use "somewhat unimportant" or "not very important" in the same context.

Modeled, or indirect, importance doesn't require formal ratings from customers. Here the assessment is based on the presumption of a relationship between the score customers give an attribute or transaction and the score they give an overall performance measure, such as loyalty or satisfaction. If expectation-related attributes (that is, the number of minutes for service) have not been accurately determined beforehand, this may confound modeled importance somewhat.

Indirect models are linear in nature in that the relationship also presumes that if ratings for individual attributes change, there will be a corresponding change in the overall performance measure. Sometimes, delivery of a product or service is highly complex in nature—such as consulting services or technical industrial testing equipment—so modeled importance must be used carefully. Also, certain customer segments in any company may rate their satisfaction or loyalty at very high levels. Somewhat like a lack of discrimination on attribute importance ratings, uniformly high overall ratings makes generating an indirect importance model more of a challenge.

Experience strongly suggests that direct and modeled importance both belong in models because they each provide their own unique value, so we typically include each. We also develop a visual model that incorporates both at once.

Customer Action Window^{SM}

Customer Action Window^{SM} is a quadrant analysis model in which direct attribute importance ratings or levels are displayed along with ratings of performance or quality. This model has been used for many years.

Earlier it was demonstrated that using mean scores can present a different, sometimes bland or less actionable, picture of customers' ratings. Although mean importance and performance ratings are occasionally used (largely in situations where clients have been reporting data this way for some time and management *expects* to see mean scores), more often the percentage of customers rating attributes or transactions high on importance and high on performance is used.

Data in all three models are presented in a quadrant format (hence the term *window* to describe it). Importance is shown along one axis of the quadrant and performance is shown along the other. Data are displayed on a median basis, that is, attributes are divided in half according to their relative performance and importance scores. This enables performance and importance of each attribute to be shown on a relative or comparative basis to each other.

The Customer Action Window^{SM} is shown in Figure 9.5. Data in the Customer Action Window^{SM} can be interpreted as follows:

- *Upper left quadrant—high attribute importance scores/low performance scores.* The customer wants it (the product or service attribute), but does not get it. Relative to all other areas of performance, this is where the company has the lowest level of perception, and these attributes should be most actively considered for improvement.

Source: ARBOR, Inc., 1991.

Figure 9.5. Customer Action Window[SM].

- *Upper right quadrant—high attribute importance scores/high performance scores.* The customer wants it and gets it. These are high profile attributes that the company performs well. They should continue performing at this level (as long as the attribute or transaction is important to the customer).
- *Lower right quadrant—low attribute importance scores/high performance scores.* The customer doesn't want it and gets it anyway. Such attributes may be cost-of-entry type basic requirements or low expectation attributes. They also may not have been communicated properly by the company so customers don't fully comprehend or appreciate their value. Sometimes, the company continues to perform well on attributes the customer doesn't care about because *management* thinks it's important. This is another example of customer-provider perceptual gap.
- *Lower left quadrant—low attribute importance scores/low performance scores.* The customer doesn't want it and doesn't get it. If possible, the company may consider eliminating such attributes, but certainly they may want to allocate fewer resources to them.

As an example of the Customer Action Window[SM] introduced in chapter 5, a hypothetical industrial products company includes twelve product and service performance attributes in its customer measurement system. Relative to all the other attributes, "product quality/defect rate" was considered the most important and had the lowest performance rating. It should receive consideration as the first priority for improvement. "Product modification flexibility" and "customer service/responsiveness" are also improvement candidates.

"Delivery flexibility," while done well, was not seen as having much importance. Perhaps the company has not communicated its value to customers; perhaps its importance has changed over time.

"On-time product delivery," "salesperson support/need anticipation," and "price" were seen as well-performed, important attributes. The company should reinforce effort on these attributes.

In attributes of low performance and low importance, one stands out: "proximity of shipping points." The company had customers all over the country, but most were along the East Coast. While they had several distribution terminals, the closest to these East Coast customers was Pittsburgh. Since this distance had only negligible impact on costs, delivery timing, and shipment flexibility during the company's 25 years in business, it was not an important consideration. Still, there was the low rating to consider. This will become more meaningful when the Dual Importance Window[SM] and Customer Motivation Window[SM] are discussed.

The industrial products company's Customer Action Window[SM] data are shown in Figure 9.6.

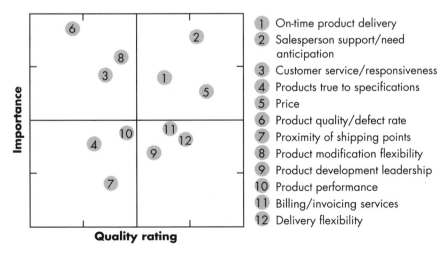

Source: ARBOR, Inc., 1991.

Figure 9.6. Industrial product company's Customer Action Window[SM].

Dual Importance Window^{SM}

The Dual Importance Window^{SM} provides a bridge between the Customer Action Window^{SM} (direct importance) and Customer Motivation Window^{SM} (modeled importance). It enables a company to identify what attributes their customers rate as important and, at the same time, see how the attributes differ in importance when modeled on an overall performance measure (such as customer loyalty or satisfaction). The upper right and lower left quadrants read similarly to the Customer Action Window^{SM}—the attributes are either truly important or truly unimportant.

The upper left quadrant and lower right quadrant set up in a similar way to attribute performance in the Kano model (see chapter 1). Attributes in the upper left quadrant are those that are low in directly rated importance but high in relationship to an overall motivational evaluation, such as intended future purchase. Attributes in the lower right quadrant have received high directly rated importance scores but do not correlate well with the motivational evaluation. These are expected, or cost-of-entry, attributes such as service guarantees or industry-standard product performance.

The Dual Importance Window^{SM} is illustrated in Figure 9.7.

The Dual Importance Window^{SM} provides several important benefits as a company evaluates attribute importance and improvement priority.

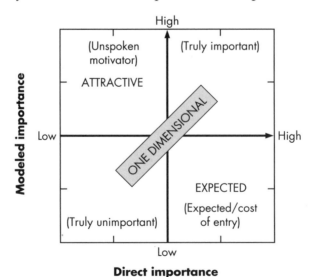

Source: ARBOR, Inc., 1991.

Figure 9.7. Dual Importance Window^{SM}.

- The identity and relationship of truly important and truly unimportant performance attributes are confirmed, giving the company better-grounded direction.
- Unspoken motivators are identified. These represent areas of attention and caution for a company because they can be either positively or negatively influencing an overall measure, such as future purchase, and, because they are attributes that had received low direct importance ratings. A company using only the Customer Action Window[SM] would not have known this.
- Expected or cost-of-entry attributes are identified. For a company in the home pizza delivery business, for instance, 30-minute delivery is highly important (direct rating) to customers, but, because *all* companies in the business offer this guarantee, it is now expected and is not a differentiator, or motivator, of purchase or high perceived overall performance.

For the industrial products company in our example, it can begin to really focus on fewer attributes. "On-time product delivery," "customer service/responsiveness," and "product quality/defect rate," while important to its customers on a direct rating basis, are actually expected or cost-of-entry attributes. The company must provide them at least at competitive levels, as a means of keeping customers. The company could, if desired or if considered a strategic opportunity, offer services and products enough above industry standards or expectations that they give the company some competitive advantages. This will, however, require an investment of resources, so it should be studied or considered further.

Among the unspoken motivators, "proximity of shipping points" stands out as an area of jeopardy (or opportunity). It has received low direct importance scores but correlates highly with future purchase intention. (See Figure 9.8.) Its full impact will be shown in the Customer Motivation Window[SM].

Customer Motivation Window[SM]

In true mathematical terms, the Customer Motivation Window[SM] is a correlation or simple regression model, in which the score on each performance attribute (independent variable) is correlated with an overall performance measure, such as intended future purchase or recommendation (dependent variable), to see how well they align. For each customer, the degree of alignment can be high (if, for example, the attribute gets a high attribute performance score and there is

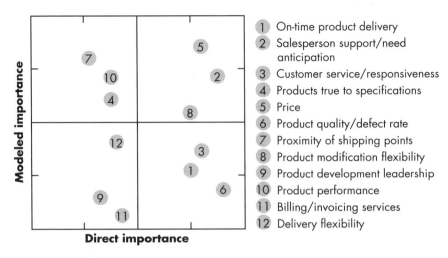

Modeled importance

Direct importance

1 On-time product delivery
2 Salesperson support/need anticipation
3 Customer service/responsiveness
4 Products true to specifications
5 Price
6 Product quality/defect rate
7 Proximity of shipping points
8 Product modification flexibility
9 Product development leadership
10 Product performance
11 Billing/invoicing services
12 Delivery flexibility

Source: ARBOR, Inc., 1991.

Figure 9.8. Industrial Products Company's Dual Importance Window[SM].

a corresponding high overall performance measure evaluation, or if the attribute gets a low performance rating and there is a low overall performance measure rating), moderate, low, or even negative (if the attribute gets a very high performance rating and the overall measure gets a very low rating).

The dependent variable most representative of motivation leading to action is purchase intent, or loyalty. There are some situations, such as health care coverage provided by an employer, in which customers have only limited choice. There are other situations, such as electrical service or local telephone service, in which customers have no choice at all. In these instances, it may be more feasible to use overall performance as the dependent variable or to rely more on the Customer Action Window[SM] for guidelines.

Importance in the Customer Motivation Window[SM] is calculated by the degree of correlation between individual attribute ratings and the overall performance measure rating. This is done for each customer, and modeled importance is the relationship of the attributes with how well they correlate with the overall performance measurement rating for all customers or a customer segment.

Just as this book is not about psychological theory, it is also not meant to be an exposition of sampling procedures and statistical analysis. In making the Customer Motivation Window[SM] a useful evaluation device, companies need only ask two questions about the application of this model.

- How many customers are needed to stabilize the model?
- How many customer segments will be actively needed or applied to decision making?

The second question should actually be answered first. Companies segment their customers based on how they market, sell, and service them. Perhaps this is geographic region, volume of business, demographic group (age, sex, income, occupation), or other customer characteristic.

The first question requires a bit of explanation. Again, without getting into such statistical details as levels of confidence, statistical significances for single sample or multiple samples, and so on, we find that customer segment samples of at least 75 to 100 respondents are sufficient to stabilize the Customer Motivation Window^{SM} model. Larger samples will provide greater data accuracy and confidence, if a company feels that is needed.

Importance and priority is expressed by placement of attributes in quadrants on a graphic. Quadrants can be described as follows:

- *Upper left quadrant—low attribute performance scores/high correlation with negative intended action (likelihood to remain loyal).* The low attribute performance ratings closely relate to low likelihood to remain loyal, so the company must target attributes in this quadrant for improvement.

- *Upper right quadrant—high attribute performance scores/high correlation with positive intended action (likelihood to remain loyal).* These are attributes of high (probable) positive leverage for the company that they should continue to emphasize.

- *Lower right quadrant—high attribute performance scores/low correlation with positive intended action (likelihood to remain loyal).* These attributes, while performed well, have relatively little leveraging impact on motivation for intended action. This may be a communication issue for the company or it may simply be one of those expected attributes that must be performed but need not be improved.

- *Lower left quadrant—low attribute performance scores/low correlation with negative intended action (likelihood to remain loyal).* These are the attributes that provide little value to the customer or the company. If possible, the company should downscale or even eliminate activities in these areas. Though not well performed, customers are relatively unlikely to miss them.

The Customer Motivation Window^{SM} is shown in Figure 9.9.

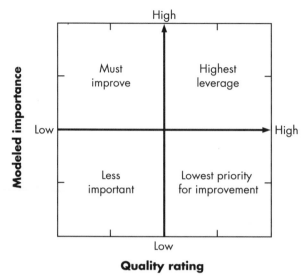

Source: ARBOR, Inc., 1991.

Figure 9.9. Customer Motivation Window^SM.

The industrial products company can now isolate the potential loyalty impact of an attribute like "proximity of shipping points." Most of the company's customers are on the East Coast; and, although this attribute was not very important on a direct rating basis, when correlation analysis was applied, it was shown that this degree of distance could cost the company business in the future. Perhaps competitors have terminals closer to these customers and this has had a motivational effect on proximity expectations. This certainly merits further consideration and study.

The company's Customer Motivation Window^SM data are shown in Figure 9.10.

For the real-life industrial products company used in our example, application of Customer Action Window^SM, Dual Importance Window^SM, and Customer Motivation Window^SM had a particularly happy result. After further evaluation, the company purchased a distribution terminal on the East Coast, almost at the mid-point of most of its customers. It not only retained current customers, it was able to use this new terminal's location for sales and marketing leverage with prospects, and it reacquired a number of major lost customers on the East Coast. The research investment to obtain this direction was minimal against the value of the result.

Source: ARBOR, Inc., 1991.

Figure 9.10. Industrial products company's Customer Motivation Window[SM].

An Additional Model Approach to Consider

If companies have adequate numbers of competitive attribute performance ratings (from their current customers, former customers and/or competitive customers), they can construct a variation of these models.

The Customer Action Window[SM] and Customer Motivation Window[SM] can also show competitive comparisons, indicating where the company has leverage against, is at parity with, or is vulnerable to competition. This is a powerful additional technique, particularly as the company is setting competitive strategy.

For our industrial products company, it shows, for example, that, not only is it performing poorly on the most important attribute of "product quality/defect rate," it is vulnerable to competition on that attribute. On "on-time product delivery," while it is doing well on this important attribute, it is equal to the competition. On "proximity of shipping points," where it has already seen potential impact on loyalty, its vulnerability to competition makes this more of a priority.

The competitive version of Customer Action Window[SM] is shown in Figure 9.11. Similar competitive readings can be taken with the Customer Motivation Window[SM].

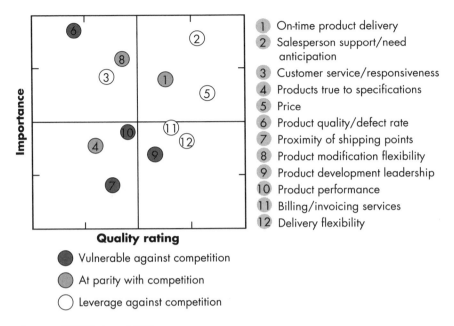

1 On-time product delivery
2 Salesperson support/need anticipation
3 Customer service/responsiveness
4 Products true to specifications
5 Price
6 Product quality/defect rate
7 Proximity of shipping points
8 Product modification flexibility
9 Product development leadership
10 Product performance
11 Billing/invoicing services
12 Delivery flexibility

⬤ Vulnerable against competition

⬤ At parity with competition

○ Leverage against competition

Source: ARBOR, Inc., 1993.

Figure 9.11. Customer Action Window^SM competitive version.

Exercise

After evaluating data from the customer measurement system using the modeling techniques, you determine that there is a high correlation between modest performance and low loyalty likelihood on "friendly/courteous teller service" in one of Twentieth Century National's city regions and one of the suburban regions. Yet, on direct importance ratings, it is one of the least important attributes. What does this information mean to Twentieth Century?

Summary

Companies use a number of data analysis techniques to understand and interpret information from their customer measurement systems. Many are limited in application. With the mission of keeping customers, companies must identify interpretive models that support this goal. Customer Action Window^SM, Dual Importance Window^SM, and Customer Motivation Window^SM help companies act on the relationship between attribute performance, attribute importance, and customer loyalty.

Notes

1. J. M. Juran, *Juran on Planning for Quality* (New York: The Free Press, 1988), 50.

2. Frederick F. Reichheld, "Loyalty-Based Management," *Harvard Business Review* (March–April 1993), 71.

3. John A. Goodman, Scott M. Broetzmann, and Colin Adamson, "Ineffective— That's the Problem with Customer Satisfaction Surveys," *Quality Progress* (May 1992): 36.

Chapter 10

Effectively Deploying Customer Data Throughout the Organization

How can you get very far, if you don't know Who You Are? How can you do what you ought, if you don't know What You've Got? And if you don't know Which To Do of all the things in front of you, then what you'll have when you are through is just a mess without a clue. Of all the best that can come true if you know What and Which and Who.[1]
—Benjamin Hoff, *The Tao of Pooh*

Once you've got the data, use them. Departments need every scrap of raw data relevant to their own parts of the business.[2]
—Richard C. Whiteley, *The Customer-Driven Company*

Planning for Deployment

The Malcolm Baldrige National Quality Award defines deployment as "The achievement of excellence by all work units in all processes and activities, in all products and services, and in all transactions with fellow employees, customers and suppliers."[3] How does a company reach that exalted and enviable state of achievement? The answer is both simple and complex.

The final objective of excellence can be reached through a plan and process for deployment. Before the process can be initiated, the deployment plan must be carefully and painstakingly developed and tailored to the company's structure and culture. As swordmaster Miyamoto Musashi said, "Step by step, walk the thousand mile road."[4]

Deployment actually begins by recognizing three things—the types of data available, where and how the data are to be deployed, and who will deploy them. The company will certainly want to make certain it has actionable data that can be applied to specific solutions.

Then the company will want to have a process owner, that is, an individual or group (cross-functional, functional, or diagonal slice) who will have overall responsibility for carrying out activity. The team may, of course, also include customers, as appropriate, in partnership for action. Selection of the process owner is as important as the information and methods of deployment. Four questions should be answered.

- Which individual or group impacts the problem/opportunity?
- Who is impacted by the problem/opportunity?
- Which individual or group has the requisite command/knowledge of organizational resources to meet objectives?
- Who is closest to the opportunity?

This last point refers to having deployment managed at its lowest possible organizational level. When the company works on a problem/opportunity, it is best to have those manage and act on solutions who have at once the most investment and the most knowledge about it. Otherwise, the process will be managed by absentee landlords, and the cultural support for change and opportunity will be greatly diminished.

The next step is formulation of the problem statement itself. Defining the problem and objective will often guide formation of the methods to take action.

Finally, companies can define a specific method to reach solutions or objectives. In the TQM world, these are called problem-solving step models. While the number of actual steps may vary, they will certainly include

- Opportunity identification
- Team formation/project scope definition
- Current process analysis
- Meet and define opportunities/outcomes
- Propose solutions
- Test solutions
- Define and implement solutions
- Track progress/change rate
- Recognize team effort/communicate results

The Role of Research in Deployment

Having adequate and actionable customer data is essential to an effective deployment plan. While it is desirable to have as many staff members as possible regularly (or at regular intervals) interface directly with customers, this is not always possible or cost-effective. Deploying the customer's message down to the lowest staff level gives the research findings life within an organization and allows all staff members and functions to gain the opportunity to better understand customer needs and concerns.

Customer information can come from many sources and locations from both inside and outside the company, but a constant source of valid customer input offers the company priorities and aids to judgement in providing better products and services.

Customer research not only provides quantitative direction but can give rich verbatim and anecdotal information on customer feelings, such as:

- Areas requiring improvement
- Registered and latent complaints
- Reasons for high/low likelihood of continuing as a customer
- Reasons for recommendation/nonrecommendation

Properly designed, analyzed, and reported, customer research is the storyline in the company's novel of product and service delivery. With each wave of research, another chapter is added.

Data Deployment Methods

In *Customer First*, Denis Walker cautioned and advised companies

> Research in itself achieves little unless there is an effective means of feeding back the data to those in the organization who can do something about it, and unless corrective action can be taken. Data must be presented in such a way as to command attention and result in action. It should also be appropriate to its audience and lead naturally to setting up challenging but achievable targets for improvement.
>
> Because little attention is paid to these aspects, much research and performance data remain unread. A mechanism which enables service managers and providers to note and discuss data needs to be established. Simply sending out a monthly report or a memo to do better in the weaker areas is unlikely to result in change. The data provides a real opportunity for staff to become involved in improving services and monitoring the effort. This leads to a sense of collective responsibility for service performance.[5]

The company can apply a two-element checklist to make certain that customer data are (or will be) appropriately deployed.

Use the Right Techniques to Reach Improvement or Solutions

Application of step models already discussed or tools like QFD or Hoshin can help ensure that customer data are deployed. With Hoshin, the company develops long-term plans around a customer-driven vision. Data contribute to refining and moderating the vision. Managers are then given tightly defined objectives, and, vertically, they deploy the objectives, develop their own tactical execution plans, set up periodic reviews, and report their progress back to management (on a semiannual or annual basis) to make certain that results are consistent with company vision, plans, and objectives (see Figure 10.1).

Hoshin actively uses customer information in developing the vision, long-range plans, and annual objectives. Customer-need priorities are then deployed within teams set up by managers. Customer-identified problems are recast as opportunities, causes are determined, and corrective or improvement activities are planned. In Hoshin, managers are expected to coach, recognize, and reinforce employees. Employees are given the freedom to take action (within context of the plan).

The values of Hoshin are that the company can make improvement breakthroughs on an ongoing basis, gain commitment to its objectives and plans, improve the process through built-in reviews, and have employees that are focused and empowered to proactively address customer needs.

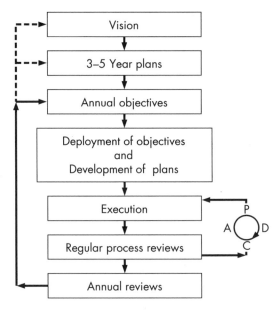

Source: Bob King, *Hoshin Planning: The Developmental Process* (Methuen, Mass.: GOAL/QPC, 1989.

Figure 10.1. Hoshin planning process.

QFD, somewhat differently, begins with a large database of customer needs and product/service/image attributes, pares the needs to a workable number, and has the customer prioritize the needs according to importance. A team (usually cross-functional in nature, compared to vertical for Hoshin) considers the customers' priorities and develops new or improved products/services to customer requirements.

The essential difference between Hoshin and QFD approaches is that Hoshin will involve the entire company, or large portions of it, in strategic process breakthrough, whereas QFD may have more limited staff involvement, and finite team assignment constructed around specific customer needs.

The company, if advanced enough, might even apply one of the newer development and decision techniques, such as Analytic Hierarchy Process (AHP). AHP takes a stated goal or objective, looks at all relevant available information (customer data, company staffing, committed funds), sets up hierarchies of detail, and then comes to a set of alternatives.

Figure 10.2 illustrates how a supermarket chain can use customer data and AHP to identify why consumers might choose one chain's store over another.

AHP facilitates group participation. Customer and other data can be presented as evidence, and all the information brought to decision analysis can be discussed and debated. The process is the crucible in which the data, participants' ideas, and intuitive/learned judgement becomes an alternative set of solutions. Interestingly, AHP is being used to both identify courses of action and assess their impact.

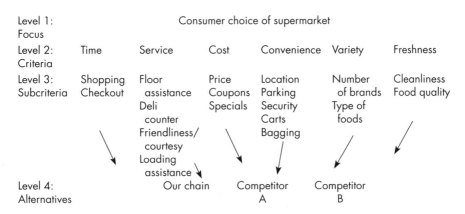

Source: ARBOR, Inc., 1993, from concepts presented in *Decision Making for Leaders* by Thomas L. Saaty.

Figure 10.2. AHP model for choosing a supermarket.

Communicate Customer Information

Communication is an often neglected area of customer data deployment and the area of greatest potential. The companies most successful at retaining customers share one common trait: They proactively deal with customer issues at the lowest possible organizational level. Whenever frontline and supervisory staff can solve, handle, or meet customers' needs and problems, they do so. Frontline contact can also serve as one source of customer information, including the identification of customer likes and dislikes and emerging customer needs. The company can determine how this direct contact information should be integrated with more formal customer debriefing, and how the various currents of customer feedback are to be converged.

As identified by Joan Koob Cannie in her excellent book, *Keeping Customers for Life*, feedback is most effective when[6]

- It is specific rather than general.
- It comes as close to the transaction time as possible.
- It focuses on behaviors and actions that can be changed (timeliness, attitude) rather than characteristics that can't be changed.
- It keys on positive improvement actions.

Companies can use newsletters, posted letters of appreciation from customers, informal update meetings for staff, and graphs showing progress against performance objectives.

When employee surveys are conducted to assess company culture or to identify perceptual differences between customer and staff, this should be broadly communicated. When customer-facing staff identify needs or problems, there should be systems in place for communicating both upwardly and cross-functionally. When companies present awards for outstanding customer service, such as trips and plaques or certificates as Digital Equipment Corporation, IBM, and The Limited do, these should have visibility though celebrations or ceremonies. These don't require size or formality, but they should be sincere. Some companies also involve customers in staff recognition. This is a particularly positive technique because it also reinforces the customer-supplier partnership bond.

The Bottom Line

Deployment may be the single most important component of a customer feedback and measurement system, yet it typically receives the least attention. Companies desiring better relations with the customer, better understanding of their needs and problems, and better proactive product and service development will have to look closely at their information and improvement network. Much time and effort may be devoted to the mechanisms for customer data collection; however, the support for collection will quickly erode without feedback processes.

Exercise

Twentieth Century National has typically communicated the results of customer studies to senior corporate and regional management for action. While individual branch service staff deal with customer complaints, problems, and needs, such information is rarely communicated beyond that branch. What can Twentieth Century do to put in place systems to improve both upward and downward deployment of customer information?

Summary

Just as in other functions dealing with generation and understanding customer information, companies must plan for deployment from opportunity statement, team formation, and solution identification. Customer research, especially data and analyses focused on retention, is central to the plan. It identifies which areas of performance should be prioritized.

Data can be deployed through application of total quality techniques and staff communication systems.

Notes

1. Benjamin Hoff, *The Tao of Pooh* (New York: E.P. Dutton, 1982), 58.

2. Richard C. Whiteley, *The Customer-Driven Company* (Reading, Mass.: Addison-Wesley, 1991), 172.

3. U.S. Department of Commerce, National Institute of Standards and Technology, Malcolm Baldrige National Quality Award, from "The Baldrige Award: Criteria that Link Customer Satisfaction with Quality Systems" presented by Curt W. Reimann at the AMA/ASQC Third Annual Customer Satisfaction and Quality Measurement Conference, Washington, D. C., April 1991.

4. Miyamoto Musashi, *The Book of Five Rings (Gorin No Sho)* (New York: Bantam Books, 1982), 52.

5. Denis Walker, *Customer First* (Brookfield, Vt.: Gower, 1990), 11.

6. Joan Koob Cannie with Donald Caplin, *Keeping Customers for Life* (New York: AMACOM, 1991), 201–15.

Kaizen and the Japanese Approach to Customer Retention: Lessons for U.S. Business

When a promise is made to Japanese consumers, it must be observed. In Japan, the customer is god.[1]

> —Taizo Watanabe, Former Director General, Public Information and Cultural Affairs, Japanese Foreign Ministry

The Japanese have clearly distinguished themselves by their attention to customers . . . their incrementalist approach to product improvement is predicated on close attention to the customer's needs and behavior.[2]

> —Kotler, Fahey, Jatusripitak, *The New Competition*

Introduction to the Concept of Kaizen

For several decades, U.S. business has studied Japanese total quality methods and incorporated a number of them into manufacturing systems and management approaches. Some have been effectively adopted in the West while others are more of a challenge. It can be argued that, owing to the current state of their economy, the Japanese system is fallible in many respects; however, their treatment of and relations with customers may be their most successful export.

The Japanese approach to customers and customer retention is a reflection of their approach to life—*kaizen.* As defined by total quality expert Masaaki Imai, kaizen, or continuous improvement, is the process by which activities reach an ever-higher state of perfection, efficiency, or effectiveness.

Kaizen is seen everywhere in Japan—in print and broadcast media and within companies themselves—where the term is frequently used as a noun or in a prepositional phrase: "The kaizen of _____." It applies to management, art, politics, trade, and, certainly, sales, marketing, and customer relations. In the United States, the term is sometimes seen in

Japanese auto plants or U.S.–Japanese joint manufacturing venture facilities and occasionally in U.S. production facilities, but few other places.

While in the West we tend to be results-oriented, prizing breakthrough-type ideas, the Japanese continue to be highly process-oriented. In this book, we needn't probe the reasons for this; suffice it to say that there are differences. Michel Greif pointed out this key difference by saying "Westerners count the golden eggs, whereas the Japanese pay more attention to the health of the goose."[3] In other words, the major value of a process-oriented approach is that it is strategic and long-term in nature.

This strategic purview is based on several components. One of these is the learning and information that leads to more customer-directed thinking, planning, and product/service development. In their recent book, *The New Competition*, Philip Kotler and his coauthors discuss how Toyota has taken its obsession for continuous updated information about customer needs and focused its efforts to both attack and maintain positions in target markets: "As strategic planners of the highest order, the Japanese aim their marketing efforts not at where the competition is situated but at where they think the battlefield will be in the future."[4] This approach reflects the revered battle strategies of Chinese general Sun Tzu, set almost twenty centuries ago. Japanese companies like Toyota understand market dynamics and customer needs well enough that new products and new services anticipate customer requirements.

Another component of the process-oriented approach is the learning that leads to greater individual productivity. The *Hagakure*, the eighteenth-century book of samurai codes, advised, "Throughout your life advance daily, becoming more skillful than yesterday, more skillful than today. This is never-ending."[5] This has not gone entirely unnoticed in the West. Echoing the *Hagakure,* in *Managing in Turbulent Times*, management scientist Peter Drucker says

> The productivity of people requires, finally, continuous learning, as the Japanese have taught us. It requires that people are constantly challenged to think through what they can do to improve what they are already doing. It requires adaption in the West of the specific Japanese Zen concept of learning: that one learns in order to do better what one already knows how to do well.[6]

Kaizen and Customer Retention in Japan

In Japan, competition for customers is keen in virtually every industry. Companies go to great lengths to attract and keep customers. In Japanese department stores, for example, employees greet customers, thank them for shopping at the store, proactively help them make purchases, and even assist with parcels and packages when customers are finished and leaving the store.

Industrial products customers are often invited into their suppliers' design and manufacturing facilities as both a means of keeping contact and soliciting their input on modifications or new products. Sales and customer service staff also invest many hours on-site with the customer, learning in detail how products and services perform.

Auto manufacturers limit the number of models that can be sold in a dealership. Instead of waiting for customers to come into a dealership, teams of dealership sales representatives are deployed throughout their community to call on individual households. They know who drives what, neighborhood by neighborhood, household by household, and their appointment schedule is prioritized by who has older model cars, will be in the market for a new car shortly, and who might be predisposed to one of their models.

Often, this process begins well before the model is introduced. And, after the sale, the representative keeps a regular schedule of personal contact with the owner, making certain that the owner continues to be happy with the purchase. If any problems arise with the dealership, such as because of a service difficulty, the sales representative will also intercede for the owner, serving as an advocate. The goal is to provide "wrap-around" service for the customer so complete that another car maker or dealership will never be considered.

In designing cars, the Japanese listen to the needs and requirements of current owners and prospective buyers, and they continuously upgrade that knowledge, seeking to provide the highest quality and value. Their approach to auto design, sales, and service is very much a paradigm for what they have done in many other industries.

Upgraded production techniques and quality procedures are only a part of their customer focus. Much of what they have accomplished comes, again, from their approaches to strategy and information. Somewhat disdainfully, the former Sony chairman, Akio Morita, said, "Americans think on a basis of ten minutes, while we Japanese plan for years ahead." His feeling was that, in the United States, planning and customer service often takes a secondary role behind tactics and quick sales.

The Japanese clearly go about marketing and service in a different way. Perhaps a good method to illustrate this is how they conduct market research.

In Japan, companies sometimes do conduct customer satisfaction or other formal customer surveys (larger firms, particularly, have marketing research staffs and use the sophisticated marketing research techniques developed in Europe and the United States); however, much of managements' marketing and service decisions are based on observation and channel monitoring, that is, hands-on research.

Much like *gunpaisha,* or strategic information gatherers in samurai times, modern Japanese managers monitor, in person, wholesalers and retailers. This gives them firsthand knowledge about product movement and response, as well as the opportunity to build relationships with intermediate customers. It also provides insight into any problems that may be developing and allows them to see how customers react to products and how they are being served. Japanese managers also closely scrutinize sales data on a monthly, weekly, or even daily basis to identify positive and negative changes that might require action on their part.

Getting close to the customer also means using sales employees to conduct telephone or mail-based research, or personal interviewing when customers come to their place of business, or, like automobile dealers, actually visiting customers and prospects. The Japanese believe more in developing hands-on understanding of customer needs, expectations, and problems than they do in most types of formal research. Data objectivity is often a secondary consideration behind the value of learning and relationship. This is *kan-ken,* the combination of intuition and judgement, reinforced by information, that leads to marketing decisions. It is often facilitated by the use of teams, collating and evaluating data in the office, collecting and comparing information in the field.

One reason Japanese sales and marketing staff can stay so close to their customers has to do with continuity. Even at a time in Japan when the concept of lifetime employment is no longer as evident (as a practical matter, it was really seen more in large companies than in medium or small companies, anyway), Japanese salespeople and marketers still change jobs far less often. This enables them to develop greater expertise about their customers, channels, and competition.

In Japan, great care is taken in the hiring and training of employees. Japanese companies realize that customer-facing employees, particularly, influence customer loyalty to a large extent. The longer the employee is with the company, the better that employee can provide for customer needs and keep the customer loyal.

Much of the core of customer retention in Japan is founded on relationships. Trust is built up over time, and, given that the provider delivers consistently high quality products and services, Japanese buyers and consumers tend to be very loyal and honest. With strong relationships, customers will also be more receptive to placing larger orders or using new products.

Japanese companies, recognizing the powerful value of staff-customer continuity, are also less likely to rotate sales employees from job-to-job or region-to-region. Instead, they find innovative ways to reward employees for keeping customers, including recognition, higher salaries, and bonuses.

Much of what Japanese companies are able to accomplish when it comes to customer retention unquestionably is a product of kaizen in marketing planning, information development, delivery quality, and relationships. The Japanese aren't perfect role models—far from it, but there is learning and application for U.S. business from what Japanese companies do.

Customer Retention Kaizen for U.S. Business

Using kaizen concepts and Japanese-style customer retention focus, we have identified 12 individual techniques that virtually all U.S. companies can apply. They will be briefly outlined here and discussed in greater detail in chapter 12.

The list of techniques presumes that, in being or becoming customer retention focused, companies can, or will, work to have a culture that supports staff (payment, training, communication, interdependence, and recognition). One of the strengths of Japanese companies, still absent in so many U.S. corporations, is the *sempai-kohai* organizational and staff cohesion identified by Pascale and Athos in their landmark 1981 book, *The Art of Japanese Management.*

Pascale and Athos examined, in detail, the roots and values of Japanese corporate approaches. In addition to strategy (allocation of resources to reach goals), structure (organization chart—functional, lattice, or decentralized) and systems (procedures and processes), Japanese companies excel in the four soft Ss.

Staff—Overall personnel categories such as technical, entrepreneurs, internally-focused, externally-focused, and so on

Style—The company culture and behaviors of management and staff in reaching goals

Skills—Abilities (leadership, technical proficiency, and so on) of staff and of the company as a whole

Superordinate Goals—The incarnation of mission as expressed by staff

Superordinate goals, in particular, frequently separate Japanese and Western companies. Staff empowerment, relationships, and leadership behaviors are interwoven with the drive for sales and profits. Pascale and Athos said, "Without a doubt, the most significant outcome of the way Japanese organizations manage themselves is that, to a greater extent than in the United States, they get everyone in the organization to be alert, to look for opportunities to do things better, and to strive by virtue of each small contribution to make the company succeed."[7] This is the concept of kaizen, and it is applied to customer relationships and retention with a vigor equal to that exercised in their other company activities.

With this in mind, the list of 12 techniques will be presented, in the order they should be considered, within a three-element structural continuum—culture, information, and action—or CIA, if you like.

Culture

Total Company Involvement in Customer Retention. Mission and vision statements are absolutely vital to a company's essence and culture. They should be much more than just words. Militarily speaking, they must be banners behind which every employee can march. Any set of statements not directly addressing the imperative of keeping customers loses the value of a strategic, total customer focus. Companies cannot expect every employee to be retention-driven if their fundamental credo doesn't specify it.

When a company like MBNA says "Success Is Getting the Right Customers—and Keeping Them" on the cover of an annual report, lists its five customer-driven, staff-supporting precepts on the inside cover, and continually communicates to staff in scores of ways that they should think of themselves as customers, it is fair to say that customer service and customer retention has come very close to becoming a corporate religion.

Everyone, from staff to suppliers and customers, understands and appreciates that level of commitment. Customers will tend to seek out, and stay with, companies that are proactive and responsive to them.

Internal Communication/Active Listening. Companies will find it considerably more of a challenge to be customer-focused if they do not practice cross-departmental communication and active intradepartmental listening. In many companies, there is so much chimney communication, informational gatekeeping, feudal management practice, and formal memo-writing that departments become isolated fortresses. Much of the emphasis is inward, protecting departmental and sectional fiefdoms, and there is little remaining energy to be customer-retention focused.

Customers are often aware of how well their suppliers communicate and cooperate within. They will gravitate to companies that are proactive, responsive, and exhibit coordination.

Strategic Empowerment and Leadership Skills. Empowerment and leadership are hot terms in corporate training circles today. They are both simple concepts, really. In *The New Competition*, Kotler, Fahey, and Jatusripitak devoted an entire chapter to Japanese strategic approaches, which are built on long-range individual and corporate commitment, flexibility, and creativity.

Strategic leadership is management's willingness to "let things happen" rather than make things happen within a defined set of parameters. Translated as kaizen, employees are responsible for themselves and responsible for customers. It is "a willingness to take risks and practice entrepreneurship; actions to put in place a strategic organization; and a mind-set that relentlessly challenges others to think strategically. These attributes typify many Japanese organizations. Without these attributes, it is difficult to visualize a top management team exerting strategic leadership within their organization."[8]

Strategic empowerment is the willingness to give staff latitude of action, in our context especially, where serving customer needs is concerned. Empowerment on behalf of the customer was exemplified in the words of the late William Gore, the founder of sport clothing manufacturer W. L. Gore: "We don't manage people here. People manage themselves. We organize ourselves around voluntary commitments."[9]

Kotler, Fahey, and Jatusripitak summarized Japanese companies' kaizen of strategic empowerment and leadership's impact on customer retention by saying[10]

> What they do in the marketplace reflects the mind-set within their organization. The incremental and emergent nature of much of their strategic behavior reflects a belief that success in the marketplace is not won overnight. It is an accumulation of minor victories, winning a long series of local wars. Continual product and market development emanates from a belief that the competitive arena is ever-shifting; competitors and customers do not stand still.

In the United States, companies like Northern Telecom practice strategic empowerment and leadership with customers. Over the past several years, its revenues, productivity, and customer service and quality ratings have risen dramatically, in part because it has actively supported staff proaction and communication within the company and with customers.

Active and Visible Senior Management. Senior management must not only set strategy and define a customer retention culture, they must live it by being in regular contact with customers themselves. For Japanese managers, this is partially done to reinforce the values and goals they set for staff, partially for market information, and partially for public relations impact.

Japanese companies regularly have senior management on-site with customers, by themselves or with teams. For smaller companies, this is a matter of pure survival. Their competitors will be deeply involved with the same customers. In Japan, initial sales and customer retention are built on relationships, and the absence of senior management from this process, however briefly, sends a signal that the company no longer values that customer's business.

The retention effect of senior management visibility cannot be minimized. In a recent *Harvard Business Review* article on senior management's marketplace involvement, Francis Gouillert and Frederick Sturdivant said[11]

> A senior executive's instinctive capacity to empathize with and gain insights from customers is the single most important skill he or she can use to direct technologies, product and service offerings communications programs, indeed, all elements of a company's strategic posture.

Information

Customer Segmentation. Japanese companies typically work with customers as individuals, proactively providing for their specific needs and requirements. Customer input and feedback is actively sought, so that suppliers can react immediately.

There is also recognition that customers can be better served if they are viewed on a segmented, clustered, niched, fragmented, or even individual basis—size, level of product/service usage, type(s) of products/services used, and demographics. This has been termed micro marketing, micro selling, or relationship marketing. Segmented customer information also gives companies strategic leverage and flexibility. They are better able to allocate resources and create more attractive products by serving customers on a niche or individual basis.

An excellent example of micro marketing is 7-Eleven Japan. At 7-Eleven Japan, the company has a $200 million system that both monitors inventory and tracks customer item preferences. And they go further.[12]

> Clerks even key in the sex and approximate age of each customer to monitor buying patterns. Orders are transmitted instantly via satellite to distribution centers and manufacturers. Anything that doesn't move is immediately discontinued: Of the 3,000 items each franchisee carries, 70% are replaced annually. A bare-bones inventory saves money, with shelf space allocated only to what local shoppers really want.

Further responding to customer needs, 7-Eleven Japan stores have become "a one stop errand center where customers can make photocopies, send faxes, develop film, and even pay utility and insurance bills,"[13] as desired, on a store-by-store basis.

Motorola, known for high quality products, manufacturing systems leadership, and superior customer service, is able to provide each of its telephone pager customers the special features and alterations they require. This has kept them predominant in the competitive pager business.

Companies considering customers as generally similar in nature will tend to have less flexible strategy, structure, and systems. This will also yield less responsive staff, with lower-grade skills, no creative communication, and blanket general customer retention goals.

Customers, as the Japanese have amply demonstrated, will gravitate to suppliers that personalize products and services.

Hands-On Research/Communication Skills Training. Customer contact is both an opportunity for reinforcing the company's competitive position and an opportunity to learn. In Japan, customer contact serves reinforcement, intelligence, and several other purposes.

Companies in the West generally do the first well, but they are rarely able to capitalize on contact to its fullest learning extent. This is because staff have not been trained in how to conduct informal, hands-on research with customers. Such research includes identifying and understanding changes in customer needs, expectations, and complaints in whatever contact circumstances arise—working with marketing channels (wholesalers or retailers), sales, engineering/design, senior management, and so on.

Just as sales staff are not born salespeople and must be trained in sales skills, so hands-on research and communication skills must be learned. As Gouillert and Sturdivant point out, this is also true of senior management.[14]

> Most top-level managers spend time visiting customers. But all too often those visits are superficial. The managers don't invest the effort needed to understand and empathize with the customer. They may have preconceived ideas about client's situation and, as a result, may not ask imaginative, probing questions or separate significant kernals of information from the overall picture.

In other words, they collect information but not knowledge.

Japanese managers and customer contact staff receive training in how to debrief customers. Some is formal, while another method is like osmosis through mentors, and some is on-the-job as part of a sales or service team. This is an integral part of their approach to market research. While not professional interviewers in the sense that full-time market researchers are, they nevertheless have been schooled in collecting knowledge. Hands-on research gives Japanese companies the ability to

- Design products and services exactly to the requirements of customers. They are organized to understand how products and services are used, to collect customer requirements data and apply them. This also means that they can better control product/service development and improvement systems.
- Handle complaints quickly and proactively generate them—positively contributing to both development and customer relations.
- Build continuous service systems around customer needs.

Many customers, particularly those in technical and industrial markets, have come to prefer a hands-on research approach from their suppliers rather than formal market research, largely because they can see tangible benefits in their participation.

Regular Direct Customer Contact. Having a regular customer contact schedule is somewhat like an insurance policy in Japanese company cultures. It supports staff training, product development, and service processes while keeping the company abreast of current customer needs, policy revisions, personnel changes, and competitive activity. This may include individual or team visits to retailers, dealers, and customers on a weekly, monthly, quarterly, or annual basis.

As previously discussed, Japanese companies typically create customer contact teams. There may be an overall coordinator, who does most of the supplier-customer relationship maintenance and has responsibility for keeping the customer. He or she visits customers on a routine basis, working with management and operations staff. Back in the office, he or she coordinates with employee product and service improvement groups, and arranges staff visits to customers to work on specific problems or to gain operational insight. Again, these visits are also the basis for generating performance feedback and competitive information.

More U.S. companies have come to realize that investing in a constant program of customer contact, and integrating the information into their own operations, both increases staff involvement and keeps the focus on customer retention.

Customer Partnership. The ultimate objective of total company involvement, relationship building, information gathering, and regular customer contact is partnership formation. Partnerships are built on trust, and they benefit both providers and customers. Partnerships are considerably more proactive and retention-focused, and, in comparison to the firefighting of many U.S. companies with their customers, communicating only when problems occur, they are less upsetting to the provider and the customer.

Japanese companies' customer teams, routinely working with the customers' own (cross-sectional) teams have well-set structures and activities. They partner to work on kaizen projects, whether in product, channel, service, accounting, order processing, or some other provider function.

An outstanding American example of partnership formation is that of Preston Trucking of Maryland. Working with customers, it formed hands-on data collection, analysis, and application teams, covering such issues as customer service, billing accuracy, delivery timeliness, and safety. With a kaizen partnership in place, Preston's revenue grew by almost 200 percent between 1978 and 1990.

Formal Research. In concert with informal hands-on, customer visit research, Japanese companies have increasingly used formal market research approaches. These include qualitative, clinic-type sessions for product and service development and surveys among customers and prospects.

While the Japanese, by virtue of organizational culture predisposition, use sophisticated research techniques less than American companies, there are increasing numbers of independent market research suppliers providing these services in Japan, and, especially among larger companies, professionals on staff to administer research programs. They understand that hard customer data and evaluation models—even simple ones—should be used in conjunction with judgment.

One key way in which Japanese companies are different from their U.S. counterparts is in data deployment. This will be discussed shortly.

Complaint Evaluation and Responsiveness. Only highly proactive approaches will encourage customers to express complaints before they become major potential defection issues. Japanese companies do this through their programs of regular multilevel customer contact. They are just as likely to collect such feedback from senior management as equipment operators. They are organized to process and respond to complaints immediately.

There have been many studies showing that once a customer has expressed a complaint, its speedy and successful resolution will tend to make that customer more loyal. Companies have often regarded complaints as criticisms instead of opportunities for improvement and so may be inappropriately organized to respond.

An ancient Japanese saying goes: "When someone is giving you his opinion, you should accept it with deep gratitude. If you don't, he will not tell you the things that he has seen and heard about you again." Similarly, customers will gravitate to, and stay with, companies that seriously listen and respond to their complaints .

Action

Active Deployment of Customer Data. Where and how customer data are deployed often makes a difference in loyalty. Japanese companies are thoroughly organized around data deployment and action. U.S. companies tend to be more selective and guarded, and not as well organized for data deployment.

In Japanese companies, customer data are deployed to employee process groups, management, and company communications media (newsletters and bulletin boards). Planning committees use the data as do staff teams developing new standards and controls.

The principal uses of customer data, however, are reflected in actions back to the customer. Product or service quality enhancements, complaint processing and response, staff-customer initiatives—all come from the flow and deployment of information. In fact, one reason U.S. and other foreign companies find such great challenge and frustration in trying to meet the needs of Japanese customers is the strong bond of relationship, partnership, and the culture of continuous information flow and responsiveness Japanese companies expect of their suppliers. Considerably more than supplier proximity, it is the kaizen culture of customer retention that involves everyone in the supplier's organization.

Teamwork. The Japanese didn't invent teamwork, but so many of the quality processes they've developed depend on teams that they have raised teamwork to a fine science. So, too, do Japanese companies apply team concepts to customer retention.

Teams are carefully formed to take advantage of individual member complementary strengths. Whether internal teams addressing customer needs, customer visit teams, or supplier-customer teams, they are empowered to identify problems and projects, chart their own performance progress, generate and try new ideas, and effect solutions. Similar to deployment training, Japanese teams are trained in kaizen and process. In the United States, teams tend to function in the short-term; in reactive, limited responsibility assignments; and with close supervision. In Japan they are self-directed and ongoing with full authority and responsibility to act.

Katzenbach and Smith studied the impact of successful teams on organizational performance, skills development, problem-solving, and communication; and they identified five characteristics possessed by superior teams.[15]

1. Small size—If a team is too large (it has more than ten members), interaction and decision making will be a challenge.
2. Complementary skills—Members possess skills such as technical, functional, interpersonal, problem solving, and decision making.
3. Common purposes and goals—There is agreement on short-term and long-term objectives.
4. Process-sharing—Task assignment, schedule development, and division of work falls equally on all members.
5. The group and individual members take responsibility *and* accountability.

Percentage of companies in four industries that consider these criteria of primary importance in compensating senior managers

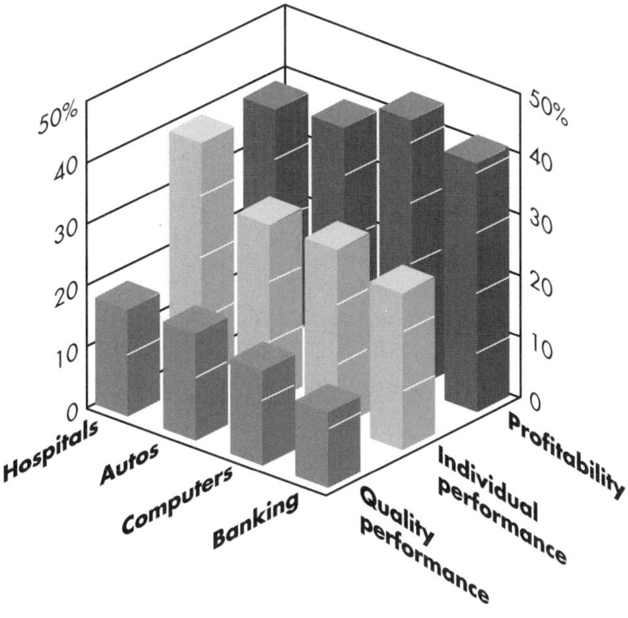

Source: Ernst & Young and the American Quality Foundation, 1992.

Figure 11.1. Quality's lagging role.

In working for such major goals as improving customer retention, teams are advised to go for small wins in product/service delivery (that is, kaizen), by training themselves intelligently and using the most current and appropriate customer needs information available.

A Final Note on Kaizen and Customer Loyalty

Kaizen in a corporate culture depends on total commitment to gradual, continuous improvement for *all* personnel and *all* processes; however, few companies have shown the discipline to make change and improvement at a controlled pace. The result, unfortunately, is that quality initiatives have either foundered or been abandoned by many companies because their goals weren't explicit or specific—such as increasing the level of customer loyalty—and they weren't seeing results.

Rather than building programs around customer loyalty, which, as demonstrated, leads to higher quality and profitability levels, companies in many industries have tended to focus on short-term profitability. (See Figure 11.1.)

In the United States, delivery and service, essential elements of kaizen quality performance among Japanese companies, have been ignored or received far less attention than, for example, cost reduction. To be global players, not to mention surviving in their own domestic markets, U.S. companies must change this mindset.

Exercise

Twentieth Century National has traditionally conducted only formal quantitative customer research. Data have been presented in reports, and the reports have been distributed to senior branch and regional managers. Twentieth Century, while concerned about what customers think, has made little additional use of the data.

Based on kaizen customer retention approaches in this chapter, what changes in organization, customer involvement, research, deployment, and training would you recommend?

Summary

Japanese companies have applied the concept of *kaizen,* or gradual, continuous improvement to all phases of business endeavor, including customer retention. This is largely constructed around approaches to learning and strategy, and translates to extremely close relations with customers.

For U.S. companies, there are 12 kaizen lessons, or techniques, they can apply to keep customers loyal. These can be divided between company culture, customer information, and methods of action.

Culture
1. Total company involvement in customer retention
2. Internal communication/active listening
3. Strategic empowerment and leadership skills
4. Active and visible senior management participation

Information
5. Customer segmentation
6. Hands-on research/communication skills training
7. Regular direct customer contact
8. Customer partnership
9. Formal research
10. Complaints evaluation and responsiveness

Action
11. Active deployment of customer data
12. Teamwork

Notes

1. Divina Infusino, "Taizo Watanabe: Japan's Voice to the World Discusses Common Ground," *Vis a Vis* (April 1992): 62+.

2. Philip Kotler, Liam Fahey, S. Jatusripitak, *The New Competition* (Englewood Cliffs, N.J.: Prentice-Hall, 1985), 252.

3. Michel Greif, *The Visual Factory* (Cambridge, Mass.: Productivity Press, 1991), 175.

4. Kotler, Fahey, and Jatusripitak, *The New Competition,* 201.

5. Yamamoto Tsunetomo, *Hagakure: The Book of the Samurai* (Tokyo: Kodansha International, 1979), 27.

6. Peter F. Drucker, *Managing in Turbulent Times* (New York: Harper & Row, 1980), 24–25.

7. Richard Tanner Pascale and Anthony G. Athos, *The Art of Japanese Management* (New York: Warner Books, 1981), 123–26.

8. Kotler, Fahey, and Jatusripitak, *The New Competition,* 256.

9. Michael W. Lowenstein, "Black Belt Marketing," *Marketing News* (7 November 1986): 10.

10. Kotler, Fahey, and Jatusripitak, *The New Competition,* 256.

11. Francis J. Gouillert and Frederick D. Sturdivant, "Spend a Day in the Life of Your Customers," *Harvard Business Review* (January–February 1994), 116.

12. Karen Lowry Miller, "Listening to Shoppers' Voices," *Business Week/Reinventing America* (1992), 69.

13. Ibid., 69.

14. Gouillert and Sturdivant, "Spend a Day in the Life of Your Customers," 117.

15. Jon R. Katzenbach and Douglas K. Smith, *The Wisdom of Teams* (Cambridge, Mass.: Harvard Business School Press, 1993), 43–64.

Customer Retention and Its Role in Total Quality and the Continuous Improvement Process

Practicing a thousand days is said to be discipline; practicing ten thousand days is said to be refining.[1]

—Miyamoto Musashi, *The Book of Five Rings*

The rate at which customers come back is the best—and perhaps the simplest—way to measure the quality of the company's products and customer service.[2]

—Peter Dawkins and Frederick Reichheld,
Directors and Boards, Summer, 1990

Constancy of Purpose and Process— A Four-Step Model

Companies wishing to incorporate continuous improvement—kaizen— in their customer objectives should seriously consider a total quality model, or system, for enacting customer retention and keeping the concept in place. Such a system should employ quality enhancement tools, customer data, and the capabilities of staff. A four-element model, the Integrated Voice of the Customer (VOC) System[SM], was developed for this purpose.

- Plan VOC (assessment)
  - Cultural readiness for customer-driven needs information
  - Assessment of information systems already available
- Gather VOC (identify needs)
  - Customer-defined needs, expectations, problems, and complaints (see chapters 4 and 5)
  - Hands-on interviewing by staff for VOC capture and/or use of professional customer research firm as partner

- Understand VOC (collect and analyze customer information)
  - Attribute performance and importance, transaction assessment, latent and registered complaints impact, and gap profiling (see chapters 6–8)
  - Prioritization modeling based on performance, loyalty, and recommendation (see chapter 9)
- Deploy VOC (take appropriate action)
  - Quality improvement teams
  - Improvement programs and follow-up measurement (see chapter 10)

This model closely approximates the Shewhart Plan-Do-Study-Act process applied to most total quality programs, but it is particularly appropriate to a customer-retention focus.

As needs identification, data generation and interpretation, and deployment have been covered in some depth, this chapter will explore the reprogrammed cultural orientation necessary to achieve optimal customer loyalty. Integral to the exploration will be incorporation of VOC System elements.

Planning for the Voice of the Customer (Assessment)

Before beginning a companywide continuous improvement, total quality initiative based on customer loyalty, the company needs to go through a checklist or assessment of its own values, strengths, and weaknesses. Many total quality programs have failed or did not meet corporate expectations because there was insufficient thinking and planning at the outset.

The values, strengths, and weaknesses include such things as

- Performance
- Flexibility
- Speed
- Staff capability/diversity
- Senior management commitment
- Senior management involvement
- Innovation
- Teamwork
- Ethics/integrity
- Empowerment

- Training
- Communication
- Policy change/action (deployment)

This assessment process may be time-consuming, even expensive, but it is certain to improve the quality of the corporate culture and the customer loyalty effort.

In addition, and just as importantly, the company should evaluate its customer information system and points of customer contact. Customer relationships, after all, range from the simple (such as consumer catalog purchases) to the highly complex (such as technical industrial products or services). The information system, to be effective, must adjust to the complexity level of the customer's voice, and it should generate information in a clear, accurate, objective manner and with the frequency needed to be current.

Traditionally, companies have developed customer information systems by looking inward, establishing a locus of customer input and feedback, processing it, and then radiating it out to sales, marketing, operations, R&D, and other groups. With an Integrated VOC System, the paradigm will be shifted to an outward focus on the customer, and the customer's voice will dictate and determine where and how information is channeled.

Without formally defining VOC, we have actually done so throughout the book. It is the needs, expectations, problems, and complaints that form perceptions (the customer's reality) and lead to intended and ultimate action. As frequently stated, satisfaction, while a part of the process, only comes into play as a yardstick of performance when the customer has a limited choice of suppliers or no choice at all. While a company may have volumes of satisfaction-based VOC *data*, few have been able to translate such data into real and sustained action.

There are two key steps involved in planning for VOC: customer identification and VOC systems planning.

Customer Identification

There are four unique types, or groups, of customers within an Integrated VOC System.

1. Internal customers
2. Intermediate customers
3. External customers
4. End users

This step begins with an understanding of who the company's *internal* customers are. Internal customers consist of functional groups, such as marketing, finance, production, and engineering, plus the collective horizontal and vertical management layers. It includes an assessment of information flow and working relationships between internal customer groups.

Next come *intermediate* customers. Depending on the type of business, this could be distribution channel elements such as wholesalers and retailers, transportation companies, and even other business units within the same company. Information generally flows back and forth between internal and intermediate customers; however, the amounts and types of information, and groups involved in receiving and using information, may vary considerably. There is a tendency for intermediate customers to have less voice than other customer types, with little identification of their needs and problems.

Finally comes the *external* customer, usually the ultimate user or end user of company products and services. The word *usually* is applied to external customers because they can range from simple to complex. A consumer purchasing dishes at a department store can be considered both the external customer and end user; however, airlines or restaurants purchasing the same dishes are the external customer, but not the end user—their customers are.

Customer identification then extends to segmentation, and segmentation has several levels. First, how is the company organized to respond to intermediate and external customers—by business or market, size, or geographic area? Within each of these segments, for example, who are the contact points and decision makers, and what are their unique perceptions and needs? Customers can be further segmented by type, such as purchasing agents or engineers in business-to-business settings, and by frequent/infrequent, younger/older, or male/female buyers in consumer markets.

In the world of total quality, customers should be viewed as a *process*, much like development and delivery of products or services. Communication and relationships are integral to the customer process, and, as part of planning, companies should determine where they have communication alignment and misalignment breakdowns between internal, intermediate, and external customers.

Each group, after all, impacts relationships with the customer, both directly and through their relationship with other internal groups. This concept is called *suboptimization,* and it seeks an understanding of cross-departmental effectiveness and how well each group meets customer needs.

Companies can actually create their own case studies as instructional exercises to determine (1) the accuracy and utility of customer segment definitions (and agreement on those definitions within the company), and (2) how they (and their customers) view communication and relationship alignment.

VOC Systems Planning/Assessment

Before building on the existing VOC systems, companies should first conduct an assessment, or analysis, of all current information system components to identify and act on opportunities for improvement.

The purpose of the assessment is to gain an understanding of the current state of the VOC processes within the organization. Through a complete analysis of these channels to and from the customer, specific improvements can be found. These improvements may range from upgrading customer listening skills through frontline training to adding tools for analyzing data collected during regular customer visits.

Without this assessment, VOC processes may remain unintegrated, haphazard, random, and uncoordinated. In addition, the assessment will allow for VOC strengths to be recognized and shared throughout the organization. This in turn should increase employee buy-in and support, essential in building a customer loyalty focus.

As appropriate, companies can involve customers in this assessment. The benefit of this is a deepening of relationships and partnership with the customer. The downside is that it may expose a weakness in the relationship before the company is set to act on changing that part of their system.

The assessment process can range from simple to complex, depending on the VOC systems currently in place, the type of business or businesses involved, and the level of interaction and information flow within the company and between company and customer. The assessment's product will be a determination of improvement opportunities and directions for VOC systems. Are there, for example, problems with VOC documentation, analysis, and dissemination? Are any customers partially or wholly out of the VOC system loop because of size, market, or location? Do resource restrictions or corporate culture act to constrain VOC systems?

When assessment, considered as a process, helps the company address specific opportunities for improvement, the remainder of the integrated plan to gather, understand, and deploy customer information can emerge. These opportunities include a prioritization of VOC system elements to upgrade, a sense of the scope of work involved (staff, time, money, and facilities investment), a validation that, indeed, VOC system improvement opportunities exist, and a platform from which to allocate and assign resources. The assessment will also pinpoint criteria representing improvement or solution.

The company plan will state what the current VOC system looks like, what an improved VOC *should* look like, and how the company will reach the reconfigured system objective. In fact, the plan will cover who is involved (process owners or coordinators, customers), what will be done, specific system elements to be included, where it will be done (pilot or incubator project, single division or department, or entire company), when it will be done (timeliness), why it will be done (objectives stated as benefits), and how it will be done (resources, cost).

Before moving forward to the gather element of the VOC system, the company should

- Develop purpose, or objective, statements.
- Identify knowledge gaps.

The purpose statement should address what information the company needs to have from customers in order to optimize loyalty. It should describe what specific actions or decisions the company can make (or wants to make) with the data. It should also integrate how new information or learning will fit into, or change, current VOC systems. Having a purpose statement will also, and perhaps most importantly, guide all VOC activities, helping ensure coordinated activity and commonality of effort.

Knowledge gap identification requires that the company identify, as finitely as possible, what they currently know about customers, what they need to know, and see that knowledge in the context of their current VOC systems. After all, there can be a little or a great deal to know about customers, but only certain areas of knowledge are pertinent to the goal of keeping customers.

When this element of assessment has been completed, the company will

- Understand the current state of customer knowledge and its own ability to gather necessary information.
- Determine if the needed customer knowledge is available, either currently or with modifications of its VOC system.
- Develop a plan to bridge the knowledge gaps.

The plan will help the company chart the process of *who* is involved, *what* information is required and collected, *when* it is collected, *where* it is collected (location and method), *why* it is needed, and *how* it will be applied and used, that is, what decisions it will support.

Gathering the VOC
(Identifying Needs)

Coming from the foundation of the VOC system plan, the company will have a scope of what retention-centered information is required. This, in turn, will facilitate an allocation of resources (staff, time, culture, confidence level required) and an understanding of the impact of gathering VOC on *all* the company's customers—internal, intermediate, and external.

Resources and scope, combined, will define methods used to gather VOC. If the scope of information is equal to or less than the company's resources and constraints, gathering can proceed quickly. If the scope is greater than available resources, the company may need to do more fine-tuning to the customer information plan, such as modifying VOC systems or gathering VOC in stages.

As discussed in chapters 4 and 5, the objective of gathering VOC is to identify customer needs, expectations, problems, and complaints. This information is then translated into attributes, transaction statements, and other measures that will help to prioritize customer loyalty–focused activities. There are three methods the company can use to gather VOC.

1. Active (proactive) methods
2. Receptive (reactive) methods
3. Indirect methods

Active, or proactive, VOC gathering methods are those in which the company goes directly to the customer or to customer venues. These may be site visits/plant tours, trade shows, or industry conferences where information can be generated on an informal basis. Or, the company may choose to use more formal qualitative techniques, such as personal, in-depth interviews; focus groups; or limited, objective minigroups. Formal qualitative research can be conducted by a third party, such as a research supplier or consultant, or it can be hands-on, in which company staff, trained by a total quality or market research facilitator, conduct the research themselves (as part of a team or with consultants). VOC can also come from quantitative research, especially from rich verbatim data (reasons for low performance ratings or unexpressed complaints).

Receptive, or reactive, VOC gathering are those situations in which the customer comes to the company to provide information. This includes registered complaints (see chapter 4), product returns, solicited or unsolicited suggestions, and supplier audits done by the customer.

Receptive VOC gives the company some tactical opportunities to enhance customer loyalty. First, when the customer has voiced a problem or complaint and the company resolves the issue (particularly if it is done courteously, completely, and efficiently), numerous studies have shown that this customer is often more loyal than customers who have not expressed a complaint. Sometimes, even acknowledging to the customer that the company is actively listening and acting on concerns is enough to increase loyalty.

The proactive company uses receptive VOC gathering opportunities to focus on capturing the detail of customers' input and for identifying or creating preventive countermeasures. The customer frequently controls both the frequency and type of receptive information given to the company. To optimize the value of this information, the company can also validate it through further dialogue, examine root causes, and follow up and monitor the countermeasures.

Receptive VOC should not, however, be viewed as representative of how customers feel about the company. Too frequently, as noted earlier, companies use such input sources as registered complaints to make changes, only to find that this was a poor investment of resources because its scope was too narrow.

Indirect VOC gathering methods, the most subtle of the three, include company examination of a specific customer action. That action may be increased business, less business, new business, customer defection, or a change in a customer requirement, such as quality level or delivery scheduling. To keep any customer action from being viewed either passively or with alarm, indirect VOC inquiry instead can be built into the company's overall VOC system, that is, having any change in the customer's status be a stimulus to VOC gathering.

In the previous chapter, 12 techniques within three elements were presented that would, if applied, help a company move toward kaizen in its customer retention efforts. Those dealing with listening and questioning skills are particularly important in gathering VOC. Anytime the customer is in a VOC gathering situation, objectivity on the part of the company or the company's agent is paramount. Care must be taken to ensure that questions are not theoretical, leading, or confusing to the customer. After all, the company will benefit from learning what is *actually* happening, that is, the customer's perception of reality, rather than what the company thinks ought to be happening.

Note-taking should be very accurate, with all data captured, including verbatims, and key words and phrases. One device of great use here is the verbatim card (or as termed here, Verbatim Analysis

Question
Verbatim
Context of VOC

Source: ARBOR, Inc., 1994.

Figure 12.1. Verbatim Analysis Card^{SM} example.

Card^{SM}), which enables the interviewer to isolate and segment customer statements (see Figure 12.1).

Questioning customers is both an art and a science. VOC gathering should be done in as much depth and detail as possible, including a mix of open-end and closed-end (yes/no, agree/disagree) questions. In getting to root customer needs, expectations, and problems, the interviewer also uses other devices such as creating scenarios of usage for the customer to discuss.

Traditionally, a company's internal and external listening skills have tended to be reactive, filtered, unfocused, and fragmented. Customer loyalty–driven listening is different: proactive, planned, focused, and purposeful. The set of skills might best be defined as holistic, integrating within the company's VOC gathering process and into the overall VOC system.

Understanding the VOC (Collect and Analyze Customer Information)

This element of the VOC system was covered, in detail, in chapters 8 and 9. Essentially, understanding VOC includes three elements.

1. Collecting and translating raw customer information—linguistic and quantitative—into ongoing and ad hoc measurement devices

2. Thoroughly analyzing customer research findings (which also includes linguistic material)

3. Making priority recommendations for deployment

Because the customer-retention oriented company is actively involved in understanding collected data, there are total quality tools available to help to expand and apply the evaluation included in an analytical report. These include affinity and fishbone charts, Pareto analyses, cause-and-effect diagrams, histograms, and tree diagrams, among others.

In *Total Quality Management*, Tenner and DeToro discussed a process model in which understanding the customer's voice can be related and applied to specific areas of improvement. This voice of the process has six elements and is an overall strategy for improvement analogous to our four-element Integrated VOC System, PDCA, plan-do-study-act, the Shewhart cycle, or the Deming cycle.[3]

1. Define problem.
2. Identify and document process.
3. Measure performance.
4. Understand why.
5. Develop and test ideas.
6. Implement solutions and evaluate.

The first two elements involve planning and creation of the VOC measurement system around specific goals. The last two involve action based on customer information, which will be covered in the next section and was discussed fully in chapter 10.

In addition to measurement, analysis, and prioritization, Tenner and DeToro recommend that understanding also include answering three basic questions. Both total quality and customer retention tools can be used to address them.

- Have we distinguished the vital few from the trivial many? This will isolate and categorize real problems, using quality devices like Pareto diagrams and customer loyalty model devices like the Customer Motivation Window[SM].

- Have we diagnosed the root causes? Just as Ishikawa looks at causes of problems rather than symptoms, so customer retention looks at real causes of potential defection—attrition—in understanding customer perceptions.

- Do we understand the causes of variation?[4] In total quality language, Deming concluded that variation comes from specific causes and that those causes can be identified and, ultimately, prioritized and prevented. The customer measurement system, assuming that it is robust enough in terms of design sensitivity, data collection frequency, and analytical flexibility, can isolate these causes of variation—such as product defects, delivery timeliness, billing accuracy, and customer service responsiveness—contributing to potential customer loss.

The principal objective of understanding the VOC is to identify real opportunities for deployment and action. Interpreting data from the customer measurement system will lead to conclusions. These conclusions can be validated by internal review, discussions with customers, comparison to other industry and company information, comparison to previously collected customer data, or more in-depth research. This is a critical point in a retention-focused, integrated VOC system, and companies will be well advised to thoroughly interpret customer data, using both quality and market research tools, before moving to actions and solutions.

Deploying the VOC (Take Appropriate Action)

Deployment involves both action and communication based on VOC. Information from customer measurement systems may be communicated to the entire company through such devices as newsletters, memoranda, reports, bulletin boards or charts, briefing meetings, or even on-site/off-site VOC conferences. In a company focused on customer retention, accurately and honestly reporting customer information, for purposes of collective improvement and not reprisal, is the ongoing proof that supports strong culture.

Everyone in the company should know who the customers are, what the customers' needs and expectations are, and how services and other performance areas are perceived. Just as customers are regularly surveyed and otherwise contacted, so should regular employee dialogue and communication and audits be conducted to check effectiveness, because staff are as important as customers in an integrated VOC system.

The principal purpose of deployment, however, is action. Customers are the inevitable recipient of deployment efforts, so the end result of a customer information system is how well it helps keep customers and increases sales and profits, not how much data the company has collected and analyzed. Customers usually have little interest in their suppliers' information systems, except when tangible benefit—action—is exhibited from it and on their behalf. Action has several components.

- Identification of a change, opportunity, or improvement process owner—individual, team, a specific group (marketing, accounting), or entire company.

- Statement of problem or opportunity—it must be precise and capable of measurement and real action.
- Use of applicable techniques, such as a problem-solving model, to reach solutions in the customers' terms.

Deployment, like any activity, must be managed. Company leaders should take the responsibility to drive improvement activities. This is best done with the guidance and direction of senior management. They will set the tone for internal VOC deployment and communication.

Because customer needs, expectations, problems, and complaints are dynamic and ever-changing, retention-minded companies will have equally dynamic sets of deployment and communication processes so they can act on customer input as soon as possible. Suffice it to say that, without such processes in place, the value of customer knowledge is greatly diminished.

A program of thorough, effective, internal VOC communication will help ensure that customer needs permeate the entire organization. Relentless, unswerving, companywide focus on customer needs, through VOC deployment, will foster a healthy culture and create customer business opportunities.

Deployment is the continuity necessary for VOC to be strategic. When all staff levels are fully aware of customer needs and dedicated to serving them, the company has the flexibility to work on product or service development, competition, improved internal systems, and, especially, customer retention.

In addition to improvement efforts, an organization's key measures, or *metrics*, should be developed by using customer information as a guide. These metrics are the means by which an organization regularly monitors its performance. Too often, they are formed in a vacuum, with the entire organization striving for goals that are not important to customers.

An example of this is a company that included on-time delivery as one of their metrics. Although the company regularly exceeded their goal of 98 percent on-time, they found that customers were giving an increasing amount of business to their competition. Only after customer research was conducted did they understand that it was really *lead time* that leveraged future purchase intent. The company then added product lead time as a key measure of their performance, and internal improvement focused on decreasing this metric that was critical to the customer.

In *American Spirit*, Lawrence M. Miller defined the role for customer retention as the cornerstone of any company's continuous improvement and total quality structure: "Excellence is not an accomplishment. It is a spirit that dominates the life and soul of a person or a corporation."[5] As has been demonstrated and discussed, a company seeking excellence will place as much value on keeping employees as it does on keeping customers. When employees are focused on customer retention and can see the results of their efforts (and that the company values their efforts), this has a culture-building effect. Communication and appropriate metrics will also support this effort.

If companies will actively incorporate an integrated VOC process into their culture, the positive spirit surrounding customer retention can produce excellence, today and tomorrow.

Managing VOC—A Recommendation to Consider

VOC obviously includes elements that can be daunting to any company. The costs involved in VOC planning, setting up a customer measurement system, internal and external communication, and follow-through on improvement activities are considerable. All of this necessitates high initial investment and requires continuity to justify that investment.

Companies should actively consider setting up a VOC department or a customer information system (CIS) department. For optimal effectiveness, the leader of this department should report directly to the company's senior executive. A VOC or CIS department shouldn't add to company bureaucracy, rather its creation should reduce bureaucracy. It would

- Manage all aspects of the company's VOC systems and processes, including
  –Assessment
  –Customer content
  –Customer measurement systems
  –Analysis and reporting
  –Deployment and training
  –Complaint/problem processing
- Plan for, and implement, modifications and upgrades in VOC systems.
- Act as the center of customer information in the company and serve as a resource for all company groups.
- Regularly interface with internal, intermediate, and external customers.

As envisioned, the VOC or CIS department would combine all the best features of gunpaisha, strategic planners, an early warning system, and a SWAT team. It would have the pulse of employees and company culture; be sensitive to shifting marketplace dynamics; be constantly aware of, and acting on, customer needs, expectations, problems, and complaints (on an individual customer basis, if desired); and ensure that all staff was customer-focused through communication and targeted training. Its responsibility would be overseeing the company's level of constancy of purpose and process. Its effectiveness would be judged by how much and how well it contributes to the company's ultimate goal—customer retention.

Exercise

Twentieth Century National has never had anything approaching an integrated VOC system. Customer data collection has been, of course, somewhat limited in nature, and, other than a small headquarters staff, many of its operational and marketing actions have been decentralized.

You recognize that to be grounded in customer retention, Twentieth Century National's culture will need to move from reaction to proaction, team orientation, and empowerment. As a capstone to what you have learned, design an integrated VOC system for Twentieth Century National.

Summary

Companies desiring to make customer retention a continuous improvement process will initiate a four-part integrated VOC system similar to PDCA, or the Shewhart cycle.

1. Plan VOC (Assessment)
   –Identify customers
   –System planning/assessment
2. Gather VOC (Identify Needs)
   –Need gathering methods (proactive, reactive, and indirect)
   –Value of verbatim information
3. Understand VOC (Collect and Analyze Customer Information)
   –Use information to identify vital, root cause situations and performance variation
4. Deploy VOC (Take Appropriate Action)
   –Communicate throughout the company
   –Have action procedures in place

Forward-thinking, retention-focused companies may want to set up a VOC or CIS department, which would be responsible for receiving, distributing, and following through on all customer (internal, intermediate, and external) information and knowledge.

Notes

1. Miyamoto Musashi, *The Book of Five Rings (Gorin No Sho)* (New York: Bantam Books, 1982), 53.

2. Peter M. Dawkins and Frederick F. Reichheld, "Customer Retention as a Competitive Weapon," *Directors & Boards* (Summer 1990), 42.

3. Arthur R. Tenner and Irving J. DeToro, *Total Quality Management* (Reading, Mass.: Addison-Wesley, 1992), 122.

4. Ibid., 118–19.

5. Lawrence M. Miller, *American Spirit* (New York: Warner Books, 1984), 51.

Afterword

Customer Retention Is a Many-Layered Thing

Why Many-Layered?

Companies, in developing their customer-retention processes and programs, or even acknowledging the value of a corporate customer retention focus, should also become aware of how many customer groups are involved.

Of course, the end customer, the final user of a product or service, is obvious. Less obvious are intermediate customers, such as wholesalers, retailers, OEMs and their staffs, and internal customers—the company's own employees. It is as incumbent for the company to learn, and act upon, their needs and expectations as it is that this be done for end customers. Internal customers will have unique and distinct perspectives on the delivery of the company's products and services. Certainly, periodic input from intermediate and internal customers should be included as part of the VOC or CIS.

Earlier it was discussed that narrowing or eliminating the perceptual gaps between providers (internal customers) and intermediate and end customers is vital. While many techniques exist to accomplish this objective, one of the more neglected is staff retention. Employee retention is highly aligned with intermediate and end-customer retention. As recently stated by Frederick Reichheld,

> The longer employees stay with the company, the more familiar they are with the business, the more they learn, and the more valuable they can be. Those employees who deal directly with customers day after day have a powerful effect on customer loyalty. . . . It is with employees that the customer builds a bond of trust and expectations, and when those people leave, the bond is broken. Companies wanting to increase customer loyalty often fail because they don't grasp the importance of this point.[1]

This means not only selecting the right employees (like acquiring the right kinds of customers), but also identifying, and acting on, ways to keep them. Methods of retention include money, recognition, training, empowerment, and exposure to/active involvement in other areas of the organization (sort of staff cross-pollination).

One company that believes in putting the emphasis on finding and keeping the right employees, is the global travel company Rosenbluth Travel. Rosenbluth believes that "companies must put their people first," and, "If we put our people first, they'll put our clients first."[2]

When staff are constantly encouraged to proactively contribute to company success and are rewarded for that contribution by concentrating their energies on customers, value is created across the board. Rosenbluth's concept of happiness in the workplace continues, "We're not saying choose your people over your customers. We're saying focus on your people *because* of your customers. That way everybody wins."[3]

An Opportunity Paradigm: The Managed Health Care Industry

In the managed health care industry, there are as many customers and customer layers as one is likely to find anywhere.

- Members—Employees and individuals who purchase health care coverage. A managed care company may have several thousand to several million members.
- Extended insureds—Families of members, who may also be called subscribers.
- Voluntary disenrolleds—Members who left of their own accord.
- Involuntary disenrolleds—Members who left because their company dropped the program.
- Governing organizations—For example, the National Committee for Quality Assurance (NCQA) who grants (or withholds) accreditation to managed care companies.
- Providers—Family physicians, medical specialists, nurse practitioners, care facilities, and their staffs. A managed care company may have many thousands of providers.
- Employers—Benefits administrators and executives who select and review the managed health care companies and interface with employee members. A national employer may have hundreds of health care insurers.
- Managed health care staffs.

Providers can be viewed as staff (whether independent or employed by the managed care company) because they are the frontline deliverers of service to members and their families. Chapter 6 presented the highly effective education and training program one managed care insurer uses with its providers to increase member loyalty to the insurer, member loyalty to the provider, and provider (and staff) loyalty to the insurer.

But what do managed care insurers do to help ensure the loyalty of their own staff, which, certainly, will impact the loyalty of employers and members? In some cases, very little. Increasingly, however, managed care organizations are initiating constructive programs for staff, such as having burnout-prone member relations employees accompany marketing or sales personnel on customer calls, thus broadening their involvement and contribution, reducing absenteeism and turnover, and making them happier and more proactive in their dealings with members and providers.

Companies in virtually any industry have similar opportunities with their staffs. If they are sincere about wanting to keep customers, they will do well to place the same degree of emphasis and focus on keeping employees. Success depends upon both.

Notes

1. Frederick F. Reichheld, "Loyalty-Based Management," *Harvard Business Review* (March–April 1993), 68.

2. Hal F. Rosenbluth and Diane McFerrin Peters, *The Customer Comes Second* (New York: William Morrow and Company, 1992), 24.

3. Ibid., 25.

Epilogue

This book is the written product of personal and professional kaizen: Interpreting customer and marketplace dynamics around the solid foundation of actual and intended behavior, not just opinion. The journey has been fulfilling from a scientific standpoint as well, since it is really the first comprehensive examination of customer retention as a total corporate focus. Mas Oyama, arguably the most outstanding martial artist of the twentieth century, has said,[1]

> If a person has chosen two or three paths to follow, though he may make considerable progress along them all, unless he narrows his efforts to one, he is likely to lose interest and switch from course to course as time passes. Such people become versatile but fail to achieve depth. The important thing is to choose one path.

As a concept, customer satisfaction has been a valuable aid to American business. It has been a rallying point for customer awareness and a quality perspective. It certainly merits gratitude and appreciation for this role. No doubt, "customer satisfaction" will continue to be the generic phrase most actively used by the business community when assessing product and service performance.

At a time when reactive corporate thinking must give way to proaction just so companies can remain competitive, however, the concept of customer retention will inevitably gain the acceptance it deserves. The sooner this comes about, the sooner business can benefit. A corporate customer retention focus yields a stronger, more pliant culture; higher levels of quality; and a more attractive bottom line. It isn't a totally new paradigm, just a simpler and better one. It is the one path to choose, with the added benefit that the map for that path is easy to follow.

Proponents of customer loyalty as an epicenter of corporate mission, though still few in number, seem to be constantly defending this concept against those who mistakenly use customer satisfaction as a replacement definition for *quality* just like many use Kleenex® for tissue, Xerox® for photocopy, or Jello® for gelatin. While the concept earns its acceptance, copy from a January 2, 1915, Cadillac Motor Car

Division advertisement in the *Saturday Evening Post* represents good counsel in this regard: "That which is good or great makes itself known, no matter how loud the clamor of denial."[2]

Armed with a proactive culture, the right information, and the right analytical techniques, a company can have both the right direction and the best map to optimize customer loyalty—in other words, an integrated process for keeping their best customers.

Notes

1. Masutatsu Oyama, *The Kyukushin Way* (Tokyo: Japan Publications, 1979), 23.

2. *Saturday Evening Post*, 2 January 1915.

Bibliography

Books

Akao, Yoji, *Hoshin-Kanri: Policy Deployment for Successful TQM*. Cambridge, Mass.: Productivity Press, 1991.

Abegglen, James C., and George Stalk, Jr. *Kaisha: The Japanese Corporation*. New York: Basic Books, 1985.

Albrecht, Karl, and Lawrence J. Bradford. *The Service Advantage*. Homewood, Ill.: Dow Jones-Irwin, 1990.

Belasco, James A. *Teaching the Elephant to Dance*. New York: Crown Publishers, 1990.

Beveridge, Don. *The Achievement Challenge*. Homewood, Ill.: Dow Jones-Irwin, 1988.

Bonoma, Thomas V. *The Marketing Edge*. New York: The Free Press, 1985.

Byham, William C., with Jeff Cox. *Zapp! The Lightning of Empowerment*. New York: Fawcett Columbine, 1988.

Cannie, Joan Koob, with Donald Caplin. *Keeping Customers for Life*. New York: AMACOM, 1991.

Carlzon, Jan. *Moments of Truth*. New York: Harper & Row, 1987.

Crosby, Philip B. *Let's Talk Quality*. New York: Plume, 1990.

Czepiel, John, Michael R. Solomon, and Carol F. Suprenant. *The Service Encounter*. New York: Lexington Books, 1985.

Davidow, William H., and Bro Uttal. *Total Customer Service: The Ultimate Weapon*. New York: Harper & Row, 1989.

Deming, W. Edwards. *Out of the Crisis*. Cambridge, Mass.: MIT Press, 1982.

Drucker, Peter F. *Managing in Turbulent Times*. New York: Harper & Row, 1980.

Fitz-Gibbon, Carol Taylor, and Lynn Lyons Morris. *How to Analyze Data*. Newbury Park, Calif.: Sage Publications, 1987.

Funakoshi, Gichin. *My Life in Karate-Do*. Tokyo: Kodansha International, 1975.

Goldratt, Eliyahu M., and Jeff Cox. *The Goal*. Croton-On-Hudson, N.Y.: North River Press, 1984.

Gray, Sir Alexander. *The Development of Economic Doctrine*. New York: John Wiley & Sons, 1961.

Greif, Michel. *The Visual Factory*. Cambridge, Mass.: Productivity Press, 1991.

Gross, T. Scott. *Positively Outrageous Service*. New York: Warner Books, 1991.

Handy, Charles B. *Understanding Organizations*. Middlesex, Eng.: Penguin Books, 1985.

Harris, R. Lee. *The Customer Is King*. Milwaukee, Wis.: ASQC Quality Press, 1991.

Heider, John. *The Tao of Leadership*. New York: Bantam Books, 1986.

Heller, Robert. *The Supermanagers*. New York: McGraw-Hill, 1984.

Herrigel, Eugen. *Zen in the Art of Archery*. New York: Vintage Books, 1971.

Hickman, Edgar P., and James G. Hilton. *Probability and Statistical Analysis*, Scranton, Penn.: Intext, 1971.

Hickman, Craig R., and Michael A. Silva. *Creating Excellence*. New York: New American Library, 1984.

Hinton, Tom, and Wini Schaeffer. *Customer-Focused Quality*. Englewood Cliffs, N.J.: Prentice-Hall, 1994.

Hoff, Benjamin,. *The Tao of Pooh*. New York: E. P. Dutton, 1982.

Holt, Knut, Horst Greschka, and Giovanni Peterlongo. *Need Assessment*. Chichester, Eng.: John Wiley & Sons, 1984.

Hosotani, Katsuya. *Japanese Quality Concepts*. White Plains, N.Y.: Quality Resources, 1984.

Ideals of the Samurai. Translated by William Scott Wilson. Burbank, Calif.: Ohara Publications, 1982.

Imai, Masaaki. *Kaizen: The Key to Japan's Competitive Success*. New York: McGraw-Hill, 1986.

Ishikawa, Kaoro. *Guide to Quality Control*. Tokyo: Asian Productivity Organization, 1982.

Juran, J. M. *Juran on Planning For Quality*. New York: The Free Press, 1988.

Katzenbach, Jon R., and Douglas K. Smith. *The Wisdom of Teams*. Cambridge, Mass.: Harvard Business School Press, 1993.

King, Bob. *Better Designs in Half the Time*, 3rd ed. Methuen, Mass.: GOAL/QPC, 1989.

Kotler, Philip, Liam Fahey, and S. Jatusripitak. *The New Competition*. Englewood Cliffs, N.J.: Prentice Hall, 1985.

Kume, Hitoshi. *Statistical Methods for Quality Improvement*. Tokyo: Association for Overseas Technical Scholarship, 1987.

Lao Tzu. *Tao Te Ching: The Way of Life*. Translated by Witter Byner. New York: Perigree Books, 1980.

Lee, Bruce. *Tao of Jeet Kune Do*. Burbank, Calif.: Ohara Publications, 1975.

Levitt, Theodore. *The Marketing Imagination*. New York: The Free Press, 1988.

Maslow, Abraham. *Motivation and Personality*. New York: Harper & Row, 1954.

Miller, Lawrence M. *American Spirit: Visions of a New Corporate Culture*. New York: Warner Books, 1981

Morishima, Michio. *Why Has Japan "Succeeded"?* Cambridge, England: Cambridge University Press, 1982.

Moroney, M. J. *Facts from Figures*. Baltimore, Md.: Penguin Books, 1963.

Musashi, Miyamoto. *The Book of Five Rings (Gorin No Sho)*. New York: Bantam Books, 1982.

Nayak, P. Ranaganeth, and John M. Vetterinton. *Breakthroughs*. New York: Rawson Associates, 1986.

Nikhilananda, Swami. *The Upanishads*. New York: Harper & Row, 1964.

Nitobe, Inazo. *Bushido: The Warriors' Code*. Burbank, Calif.: Ohara Publications, 1979.

Ohmae, Kenichi. *Japan Business: Obstacles and Opportunities*. McKinsey Company/United States-Japan Trade Study Group, New York: John Wiley & Sons, 1983.

————. *The Mind of the Strategist: Business Planning for Competitive Advantage*. New York: Penguin Books, 1983.

Ouchi, William G. *Theory Z*. New York: Avon Books, 1981.

Oyama, Masutatsu. *The Kyukushin Way*. Tokyo: Japan Publications, 1979.

Parulski, George. *A Path to Oriental Wisdom*. Burbank, Calif.: Ohara Publications, 1976.

Pascale, Richard Tanner, and Anthony G. Athos. *The Art of Japanese Management*. New York: Warner Books, 1981

Pater, Robert. *Martial Arts and the Art of Management*. Rochester, Vt.: Destiny Books, 1988.

Peacock, William E. *Corporate Combat*. New York: Facts On File Publications, 1984.

Peters, Tom. *Thriving on Chaos*. New York: Alfred A. Knopf, 1988.

Peters, Thomas J., and Robert H. Waterman, Jr. *In Search of Excellence*. New York: Warner Books, 1984.

Porter, Michael E. *Competitive Strategy*. New York: The Free Press, 1980.

Quelch, John A. *How to Market to Consumers*. New York: John Wiley & Sons, 1982.

Ries, Al, and Jack Trout. *Marketing Warfare*. New York: McGraw-Hill, 1986.

Rogers, David J. *Fighting to Win*. Garden City, N.Y.: Doubleday, 1984.

Rosenbluth, Hal F., and Diane McFerrin Peters. *The Customer Comes Second*. New York: William Morrow and Company, 1992.

Saaty, Thomas L. *Decision Making for Leaders*. Pittsburgh, Penn.: RWS Publications, 1990.

Schreier, Fred T. *Modern Marketing Research: A Behavioral Science Approach*. Belmont, Calif.: Wadsworth Publishing, 1963.

Sewell, Carl, and Paul B. Brown. *Customers for Life*, New York: Doubleday, 1990.

Shim, Sang Kyu. *The Making of a Martial Artist*. Detroit, Mich.: Shim Publishing, 1980.

Stelber, Stephen R., and William J. Kronwinski. *Measuring and Managing Patient Satisfaction*. Chicago, Ill.: American Hospital Publishing, 1990.

Sun Tzu (Sonchi). *The Art of War*. Translated by Samuel B. Griffith. London: Oxford University Press, 1971.

Tenner, Arthur R., and Irving J. DeToro. *Total Quality Management*. Reading, Mass.: Addison-Wesley, 1992.

Tsunetomo, Yamamoto. *Hagakure: The Book of the Samurai*. Tokyo: Kodansha, 1985.

Vavra, Terry G. *Aftermarketing*. Homewood, Ill.: Business One Irwin, 1992.

Walker, Denis. *Customer First*. Brookfield, Vt.: Gower, 1990.

Wallace, Thomas F. *Customer-Driven Strategy*. Essex Junction, Vt.: Oliver Wight Publications, 1992

Walters, G. Glenn, and Gordon W. Paul. *Consumer Behavior: An Integrated Framework*, Homewood, Ill.: Richard D. Irwin, 1970.

Wasson, Chester R., and David H. McConaughy. *Buying Behavior and Marketing Decisions*. New York: Appleton-Century-Crofts, 1968.

Whiteley, Richard C. *The Customer-Driven Company*. Reading, Mass.: Addison-Wesley, 1991.

Yoshino, M. Y. *The Japanese Marketing System*. Cambridge, Mass.: MIT Press, 1971.

Zeithaml, Valarie A., A. Parasuraman, and Leonard L. Berry. *Delivering Quality Service*. New York: The Free Press, 1990.

Zemke, Ron. *The Service Edge*. New York: NAL Books, 1988.

Articles, Brochures, and Presentations

Azzolini, Mary, and James Shillaber. "Internal Service Quality: Winning from the Inside Out." *Quality Progress* 26 (November 1993): 75–78.

Barrier, Michael. "A Greek with a Word for It." *Nation's Business* 76 (August 1988): 69–70.

Bitner, Mary Jo. "Evaluating Service Encounters." *Journal of Marketing* 54 (April 1990): 69–84.

Bitner, Mary Jo, Bernard H. Booms, and Mary Stanfield Tetreault. "The Service Encounter: Diagnosing Favorable and Unfavorable Incidents." *Journal of Marketing* 54 (January 1990): 71–84.

Brandt, D. Randall. "Business Trends: Focusing on Problems to Improve Service and Quality." *MOBIUS* 9 (Spring 1990): 23–31.

Cheser, Raymond. "Kaizen Is More Than Continuous Improvement." *Quality Progress* 27 (April 1994): 23–25.

Chua, Richard C. H. "A Customer-Driven Approach for Measuring Service Quality." Paper presented at the Annual ASQC Quality Congress, Nashville, Tenn., May 1992.

Dawes, Robyn M. "Finding Guidelines for Tough Decisions." *AMSTAT News* 203 (November 1993): 3–4.

Dawkins, Peter M., and Frederick F. Reichheld. "Customer Retention as a Competitive Weapon." *Directors & Boards* 15 (Summer 1990): 42–47.

Devlin, Susan J., and H. K. Dong. "Service Quality from the Customer's Perspective," *Marketing Research* 6, no. 1, 1994: 5–13.

Edosomwan, Johnson A. "Implementing Customer-Driven Quality Improvement Projects." *The Quality Observer* 1 (November 1991): 4–5.

———. "Customer Satisfaction Through Continuous Process Improvement." *The Quality Observer* 1 (May 1992): 20.

Edwards, Darrell, Daniel A. Gorrell, J. Susan Johnson, and Sharon Shedroff. "Typical Definition of 'Satisfaction' Is Too Limited." *Marketing News* 29 (January 3, 1994): 6.

Fay, Christopher J. "'Can't Get No Satisfaction?' Perhaps You Should Stop Trying." *Juran News,* Juran Institute, Wilton, Conn. (Winter 1995): 1–2.

Fuchsberg, Gilbert. "Quality Programs Show Shoddy Results." *The Wall Street Journal,* 14 May 1992, B-1, B-7.

Gale, Bradley. "Bringing Customer Satisfaction and Market Perceived Quality to Life." Paper presented at the 1991 AMA/ASQC Customer Satisfaction and Quality Measurement Conference, Washington, D.C., April, 1991.

Garvin, David A. "How The Baldrige Award Really Works." *Harvard Business Review* 69 (November–December 1991): 80–93.

Gausz, A. Beeler. "When Service Is Your Product, How Important Is Quality Management?" *Quality Update* 11 (January–February 1992): 37–38.

Gerlach, Ken. "Is Market Research Enough?" *Sales and Marketing Strategies & News* 1 (March 1991): 7+.

Goodman, John A., Scott M. Broetzmann, and Colin Adamson. "Ineffective—That's the Problem with Customer Satisfaction Surveys." *Quality Progress* 25 (May 1992): 35–38.

Gouillert, Francis J., and Frederick D. Sturdivant. "Spend a Day in the Life of Your Customers." *Harvard Business Review* 72 (January–February 1994): 116–25.

Graessel, Bob, and Pete Zeidler. "Using Quality Function Deployment to Improve Customer Service." *Quality Progress* 26 (November 1993): 59–63.

Griffin, Abbie, and John R. Hauser. "The Voice of the Customer." *Marketing Science* 12 (Winter 1993): 1–27.

Grimm, Cynthia. "Understanding and Reaching the Customer: A Summary of Recent Research." *MOBIUS* 6 (1987): 14–19.

Hayslip, Warren R. "Measuring Customer Satisfaction in Business Markets." *Quality Progress* 26 (April 1994): 83–87.

Hovey, Pauline. "Selling to the Japanese: A Learning Experience." *The Quality Observer* 1 (January 1992): 1+.

Infusino, Divina. "Taizo Watanabe: Japan's Voice to the World Discusses Common Ground." *Vis a Vis* 10 (April 1992): 62+.

Johansen, Johny K., and Ikujiro Nonaka. "Market Research the Japanese Way." *Harvard Business Review* 65 (May–June 1987): 4–7.

Kano, Noriaki. "Profit and Growth Through Quality," Paper presented at MAQIN Conference, Madison, Wis., August 1993.

———. "The Right Way to Quality." Paper presented at EOQ, Helsinki, Finland, August 1993.

Kano, Noriaki, Nobushiro Seraku, Fumio Takahashi, and Shinichi Tsuji. "Attractive Quality and Must Be Quality." *Quality* 14 (1984): 39–48.

Karabatsos, Nancy A. "Driving Home Quality." *The Quality Imperative* 1 (September 1992): 51–56.

Kilmann, Ralph H. "Why Total Quality Management Fails." *Managing* 7 (Fall 1993): 6–9.

Libey, Donald R. "Supercycles for the New Century: Customer-Focused Service Delivery." *Potentials in Marketing* 26 (July 1993): 67–68.

Lockhart, Daniel C., and Roger Tourangeau. "The Effect of Suggested Price Points on Open-Ended Price Estimates." Paper presented at Society for Consumer Psychology, APA Annual Convention, Washington, D.C., August 1992.

Lopez, Charles E. "The Malcolm Baldrige National Quality Award: It's Really Not Whether You Win or Lose. . . ." *The Quality Observer* 1 (November 1991): 1+.

———. "On Quality, the Baldrige, and Disinformation." *The Quality Observer* 1 (January 1992): 10+.

Lowenstein, Michael W. "Black Belt Marketing." *Marketing News* 21 (November 7, 1986): 10.

———. "Customer Research Reconsidered." *Sales and Marketing Strategies and News* 2 (March 1992): 9, 12–13.

———. "Customer Retention: What It Takes to Keep (and Lose) Your Best Customers." Paper presented at ASQC First Annual Service Quality Conference, Chicago, Ill., April 1992; Inc. Magazine Conference on Customer Service Strategies, Orlando, Fla., February 1993; SOCAP Conference, Philadelphia, Penn., November 1992; and ICSA Annual Customer Service Conference, New York, September 1993.

———. "The Voice of the Customer." *American Management Association Small Business Reports* 18 (December 1993): 57–61.

Lowenstein, Michael W., and Thomas R. Lutz. "Customer Satisfaction Measurement: How to Avoid Critical Mistakes." ARBOR, Inc. Brochure, 1993.

Maruca, Regina Fazio, and Amy L. Halliday. "When New Products and Customer Loyalty Collide." *Harvard Business Review* 71 (November–December 1993): 22–33.

McLaurin, Donald L., and Sharon Bell. "Making Customer Service More than Just a Slogan." *Quality Progress* 26 (November 1993): 35–39.

Miller, Karen Lowry. "Listening to Shoppers' Voices." *Business Week/Reinventing America* (1992): 69.

Myers, James H. "Measuring Customer Satisfaction: Is Meeting Expectations Enough?" *Marketing Research* 3 (December 1991): 35–43.

Nadel, Brian, and Jorge Ribeiro. "Access Japan." *Business Tokyo* 5 (April 1991): 44–46.

Nakui, Sotoshi. "Comprehensive QFD System." Paper presented at GOAL: The Third Symposium on Quality Function Deployment, Boston, Mass., October 1991.

Paich, Milo R. "Making Service Quality Look Easy." *Training* 29 (February 1992) (Reprint).

Reichheld, Frederick F., and W. Earl Sasser, Jr. "Zero Defections: Quality Comes to Services." *Harvard Business Review* 68 (September–October 1990): 105–11.

Reichheld, Frederick F. "Loyalty-Based Management." *Harvard Business Review* 71 (March–April 1993): 64–73.

Ribeiro, Jorge. "Export Experts at Your Service: JETRO." *Business Tokyo* 5 (April 1991): 47–48.

Schaffer, James C. "Quality Service Requires Teamwork, Which Requires Communication." *TWA Ambassador* (August 1993): 43–44.

Schlossberg, Howard. "Carmakers Try to Boost Sales by Satisfying Customers." *Marketing News* 25 (May 28, 1990): 2+.

———. "U.S. Firms Must Contend with Japanese Style Service." *Marketing News* 25 (May 28, 1990): 11+.

Sheridan, Bruce M. "Changing Service Quality in America." *Quality Progress* 26 (December 1993): 97–99.

Simmerman, Scott J. "Achieving Service Quality Improvement." *Quality Progress* 26 (November 1993): 47–50.

Sinha, Madhan N. "Winning Back Angry Customers." *Quality Progress* 26 (November 1993): 53–56.

Skrabec, Quentin R., Jr. "Get All Employees Involved in Satisfying Customers." *Quality Progress* 26 (November 1993): 87–89.

Travis, Kenneth M. "Price Sensitivity Measurement Technique Plots Product Price vs. Quality Perceptions." *Marketing News* 17 (May 14, 1982): 6.

Wyner, Gordon A., and Hillary Owen. "What Is Important?" *Marketing Research* 5, (November 3, 1993): 48–50.

"Does the Baldrige Award Really Work?" *Harvard Business Review* 70 (January–February 1992): 126–47.

Interviews with Japanese JETRO and United Nations trade mission staffs, 1984–1986.

Interview with Roger Taylor, M.D., Executive Vice President, Pacificare, July 1994.

Brochure from Amica Life Insurance Company, Providence, R.I., 1994.

Brochure from Key Risk Management Services, Greensboro, N.C., 1994.

New Customer brochure from Lands' End Direct Merchants, Dodgeville, Wis., 1993.

Index